The Mi'kmaq Anthology Volume 2

In Celebration of the Life of Rita Joe

EDITED BY
THERESA MEUSE
LESLEY CHOYCE
JULIA SWAN

POTTERSFIELD PRESS, LAWRENCETOWN BEACH, NOVA SCOTIA, CANADA

© Copyright 2011 Pottersfield Press

All rights reserved. No part of this publication may be reproduced or used or stored in any form or by any means – graphic, electronic or mechanical, including photocopying – or by any information storage or retrieval system without the prior written permission of the publisher. Any requests for photocopying, recording, taping or information storage and retrieval systems shall be directed in writing to the publisher or to Access Copyright, The Canadian Copyright Licensing Agency, 1 Yonge Street, Suite 800, Toronto, Ontario, Canada M5E 1E5 (www.AccessCopyright.ca). This also applies to classroom use.

Library and Archives Canada Cataloguing in Publication

The Mi'kmaq anthology volume 2 : in celebration of the life of Rita Joe / editors, Theresa Meuse, Lesley Choyce, Julia Swan.

ISBN 978-1-897426-29-6

1. Canadian literature (English)--Indian authors.
2. Canadian literature (English)--20th century.
3. Canadian literature (English)--21st century. 4. Micmac Indians--Literary collections.
I. Joe, Rita, 1932-2007 II. Meuse-Dallien, Theresa, 1958-
III. Choyce, Lesley, 1951- IV. Swan, Julia, 1955-

PS8235.I6M56 2011   C810.8'08973   C2011-902801-8

Cover art: Lorne A. Julien – *Love Dance*

Photo of Rita Joe on page 5 by Ronald Caplan

We acknowledge the financial support of the Government of Canada through the Canada Book Fund for our publishing activities and the support of The Canada Council for the Arts, which last year invested $20.1 million in writing and publishing throughout Canada. We also thank the Province of Nova Scotia for its support through the Department of Communities, Culture and Heritage.

Pottersfield Press
83 Leslie Road
East Lawrencetown, Nova Scotia, Canada, B2Z 1P8
Website: www.PottersfieldPress.com
To order, phone 1-800-NIMBUS9 (1-800-646-2879) www.nimbus.ns.ca

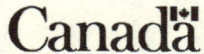

Contents

Introduction
    Theresa Meuse — 7
    Lesley Choyce — 10
    Julia Swan — 14

Rita Joe — 17

Catherine Martin — 23

Jean Augustine-McIsaac — 31

Alice Azure — 35

Denise Larocque — 45

Charles Doucette — 57

Eva Apukjij — 61

Clayton Paul — 71

shalan joudry — 80

Patricia Doyle-Bedwell — 91

Laura Johnson — 110

Theresa Meuse — 117

John Sylliboy — 130

David Marshall — 134

Mary Louise Martin — 139

Marie Battiste — 158

Peter C. Julian — 178

Robert Bernard	192
Daniel N. Paul	201
Sunset Rose Morris	213
Lindsay Marshall	227
I Wrote, Now You Write by Rita Joe	237
Lorne A. Julien	239

This volume is dedicated to the memory of Elder Rita Joe

Introduction

Theresa Meuse

In March of 2007, some of my colleagues and I gathered around the table at the Glooscap Heritage Centre in Truro, Nova Scotia, waiting for our meeting to start. It was at that moment we received news of the passing of Elder Rita Joe. All I could do was stare off in a daze, feeling saddened by the news, wondering how my mind would be able to concentrate on the meeting's topic.

I remember thinking that I never was able to personally meet Elder Rita or share a chat over a good cup of tea. Sure, I got to hear her speak at conferences or other events where she was the guest speaker, but didn't have the chance to create that one-on-one connection. So why was I feeling such a loss?

Then it came to me. Just like any other famous person who people looked up to, Elder Rita was also a celebrity who touched our hearts with her many writings and accomplishments. At that moment, I realized we had lost a valuable Elder whose wisdom was greater than many of us will ever know.

What I never got to personally tell Elder Rita was how great an inspiration she was to me. Since I was a closet writer, she gave me the confidence to think that maybe someday I too might have a story published just like she had. Over the years, I had written a few short stories from different personal experiences and always kept them in a box, hoping some day they may be useful.

That day came with the help of Elder Rita and her co-editor Lesley Choyce, who requested submissions for a new publication called *The Mi'kmaq Anthology*. Without hesitation, I sent off one of my stories for their consideration. It was not long after when I received word that my story was selected. At that moment, there was nothing that could have made me more proud of being Mi'kmaq. How honoured I felt to think Elder Rita Joe believed my story was good enough to be included in the book. Since then I have been fortunate to publish my own children's storybook, *The Sharing Circle: Stories about First Nations Culture*, and it is with great pleasure that I say it is all because of being inspired by Elder Rita Joe.

So there I sat during the meeting, thinking about Elder Rita, when an idea came to me. I could hardly wait for break time so I could tell someone about it. I remember sharing specifically with Lindsay Marshall and Dozay Christmas my notion of having a second Mi'kmaq anthology published in honour of Elder Rita Joe. They and many others at that meeting supported the idea.

When I left the meeting there was only one question on my mind: how do I begin this process? It was suggested I contact Lesley Choyce since he co-edited the first book and that is what I did. Lesley, without hesitation, gladly offered his support and together we began collecting contributions for the new book. It took a few years for us to get this accomplished, but we are so excited and proud to finally bring to you *The Mi'kmaq Anthology Volume 2*.

It never ceases to amaze me how things work out for a reason and how we may not know at the time what that reason is. I knew I wanted to share a story for the new book and wondered what that story would be. In the first *Mi'kmaq Anthology*, I shared a story about a Chief who took on the responsibility of burying some ancestral remains. For this second collection, I was blessed to have had an opportunity to bury what I believed to be the tools that might have belonged to those ancestors. Even though the book may have taken a while to complete, had it moved along more quickly, the story may not have been published. I am thankful that the delay allowed me to experience the burying of the tools and then the chance to write the story to share in *The Mi'kmaq Anthology Volume 2*.

Thank you to everyone for their written works and patience during the time it took us to get this book together. A big thank you to Lesley Choyce for his dedication in making this book become reality. And my heart can never forget to thank the Creator for blessing me with such a beautiful family and for the many gifts that come with each day.

Most of all, this book has given me the opportunity to finally say, "Wela'lin, Elder Rita Joe, for being such a great inspiration to me and many others." She will always be in our hearts and may the story of her greatness be forever passed down to each generation.

Msɨt no'kmaq

(All my Relations)

Lesley Choyce

I first met Rita Joe at a gathering of writers hosted by the Writers' Federation of Nova Scotia in the fall of 1978. She had recently published her first book, *The Poems of Rita Joe*. I had moved to Nova Scotia that year and, as a writer who had not yet published a book, I was feeling somewhat shy and out of my element. I was introduced to Rita and she said that she too was feeling nervous and out of place. As we talked I discovered that she was a gentle, intelligent woman and immediately liked her very much. She was the first Mi'kmaq person I had ever met.

We became professional friends over the years and she would come speak to my class in Dalhousie University's Transition Year Program for Black and Aboriginal students. Her graceful presence, her quiet thoughtful demeanour and her encouraging words made deep impressions on my students. It was always clear to me that Rita Joe was one of those people who was more interested in giving than taking. She knew I was involved at that point in publishing and said we should put together an anthology of Mi'kmaq writers.

And so we did.

The first *Mi'kmaq Anthology* was published by Pottersfield Press in 1997. It included seventeen contributors and it remains in print today. Near my desk where I worked at home I had posted a note Rita had mailed to me somewhere in the middle of the process when we'd been turned down for funding for the project. The note read simply, "Let's show them what we can do."

After one of Rita's visits to my university class, I walked her out to her car where her husband Frank was waiting for her. "We're going to visit the Bedford Petroglyphs," she said. Petroglyphs are images etched into rocks with stone tools that served various purposes and are often spiritual in nature. Located in the Bedford Barrens, the stone carved images were created before the arrival of Europeans on a high rock ridge that runs roughly north to south, a small record of a people and a culture that had lived here for centuries.

It wasn't until the summer of 2011 that I first visited those petroglyphs myself. Not far from the urban sprawl of housing developments and shopping centres, the trail to the site is overgrown and not well marked. The primary image of an eight-pointed star is worn down from time and weather and yet, as I sat down on the smooth rock surface, I felt a genuine sense of awe that I was here at a sacred Mi'kmaq site along the ridge that was once a well-used footpath for an ancient people. And someone had left this record behind for generations that followed. Sitting quietly beneath the blue sky with birch trees surrounding me, I remembered my old friend Rita Joe who had first told me of Mi'kmaq petroglyphs, both here and at Kejimkujik. A pair of ravens flew overhead as I traced my fingers along the lines carved into the stone long ago, thinking of the past but also the present.

Theresa Meuse had prompted me to help put together a second *Mi'kmaq Anthology*, in celebration of Rita Joe's life, and we had begun the process in 2008. Work had gone slowly and, for various reasons, we had not made significant progress but the wheels were in motion. And now the petroglyph was doing its work, reminding me that stories needed to be shared, visions recorded and poems brought to life. This visual poem from the distant past told me it was time to finish the work we had started. Now was the time.

So we got on with the job at hand. Long-time Pottersfield editor Julia Swan was enlisted to help with completion of the work – this anthology, a compilation of thoughts, images, beliefs, stories, poems and lives lived. We would like to think that Rita Joe lives on in the words here, in the work that she helped to inspire.

Rita Joe was born as Rita Bernard in Whycocomagh, Cape Breton, Nova Scotia, on March 15, 1932. She became an orphan when she was ten years old and lived in foster homes and later the Shubenacadie Residential School. As an adult, she lived in Boston before moving back to Eskasoni, Nova Scotia.

In her thirties she began to write poetry but kept it a secret until she won a poetry contest held by the Writers' Federation of Nova Scotia. Former WFNS executive director Jane Buss says of Rita Joe's writing, "Her object was to be a fine writer and take all the pain and transcend it through the stories, to transmute it into something that gave her people and her stories an honoured place."

Daniel Paul has said, "She was instrumental in inspiring people to strive for excellence in their life. She never hated anybody." Lindsay Marshall remembers her as "very laid-back, introspective, very dignified and reserved, but through her poetry she spoke volumes. She didn't let on her power."

Her books include *Poems of Rita Joe* (1978), *Song of Eskasoni: More Poems of Rita Joe* (1988), *Lnu And Indians We're Called* (1991), *Song of Rita Joe: Autobiography of a Mi'kmaq Poet* (1996), *We are the Dreamers: recent and early poetry* (1999) and *For the Children* (2008).

During her life, Rita Joe was made a Member of the Order of Canada, a Member of the Queen's Privy Council for Canada and was awarded honorary doctorate degrees from Dalhousie University, The University College of Cape Breton and Mount Saint Vincent University. In 1993, the National Film Board produced a documentary about her, *Song of Eskasoni*. In 1997 she received a National Aboriginal Achievement Award.

After suffering for several years with Parkinson's disease, Rita Joe died on March 20, 2007. A poem-in-progress called "October Song" was found in her typewriter after her death and included the following: "On the day I am blue, I go again to the woods where the tree is swaying, arms touching you like a friend, and the sound of the wind so alone like I am; whispers here, whispers there, come and just be my friend."

Rita Joe once said, "I write the positive image of my people, the Mi'kmaq." She was a poet but also a mentor and, in her own way, a spiritual guide. "When I started the first time writing," she said, "I was trying to inspire all minorities with my work. To make others happy with my work is what I wanted to do."

The varied, distinctive work of the authors included in this anthology suggests that the spirit of Rita will continue to inspire both writers and readers in the generations to come.

Julia Swan

In the classes I teach at Dalhousie University, one of the texts I regularly assign is Ojibway writer Richard Wagamese's first book, *Keeper'N Me*. This novel tells the story of Garnet Raven, who returns to his reserve as a young adult, having been taken from his family as a toddler and raised in white foster homes, absorbing along the way many unfounded negative stereotypes about his people. Garnet has to learn about his own culture one step at a time, and he is guided in this by the elder, Keeper, who was his grandfather's friend. It is a story about changing perception, as Garnet begins to discover his own history, the depth and meaning of his culture, and his vocation as a storyteller. He learns all of this because he allows himself to be taught by someone wiser than he, and he opens himself to the teachings, to gratitude, to humility, and ultimately to sharing what he has learned. A few years ago, one of my students, a young man in the engineering faculty, approached me after class to tell me how much he enjoyed this book. It gave him, he said, a new way of seeing the world – a way he had never known before. Like Garnet, he was open to a new perspective.

In my introductory remarks about this novel, I begin with Rita Joe's words from the first *Mi'kmaq Anthology*, where she describes her reaction to the prospect of compiling an anthology of Mi'kmaq writers with Lesley Choyce: "I liked that idea because we are now creating the writing instead of just being written about." I have two threads here about how Wagamese's novel ties in with *The Mi'kmaq Anthology Volume 2*. The first is that Rita Joe's words are so resonant for the fictional character of Garnet. Even in his most outlandish stories before his return to White Dog Reserve, Garnet is creating his own life and documenting it. He chooses to tell his own story. In this second volume of the anthology, in commemoration of Rita Joe, the poet laureate of the Mi'kmaq people, twenty-one writers tell their own stories – in poetry, in stories, and in personal essays. Many of the contributors here have known Rita Joe, as a family member or friend, either personally or through her writing. They tell their stories because she made it possible.

The second thread is this. As I have edited these pieces over the months of preparing the book for publication, Garnet's lessons have been before me in the correspondence with these authors, and Rita's gentle spirit has been like Garnet's Keeper, presiding over the work, teaching, sharing. It has been a humbling experience in many ways, for even in the pieces written in English, there are cadences of another language, one I do not speak, and I have tried to edit with a light hand, to preserve those rhythms. The authors have been kind in their communications with me, and patient. They have shared their knowledge and expressed their gratitude in being included in this anthology. I wish to express mine to them – wela'lin.

Where possible we tried to provide a generous amount of biographical material, but there are instances where we respected the desire of contributors to offer basic information. We also respected the choice of individual writers in the spelling of some Mi'kmaq words.

Rita Joe wrote, in the prologue to her memoir, "My greatest wish is that there will be more writing from my people, and that our children will read it. I have said again and again that our history would be different if it had been expressed by us." Here, then, is more writing from her people. There is pain in some of these stories, but there is also generosity, sharing, and teachings, if we can open our minds to new perspectives.

Rita Joe

The following works by Rita Joe were originally published posthumously in *For the Children* (with woodcuts by Burland Murphy. Breton Books, Wreck Cove, Nova Scotia, 2008). They are reprinted here with the permission of her publisher, Ronald Caplan. Mr. Caplan said in his Editor's Note to *For the Children*, "We have decided to respect the Mi'kmaq words as she left them," and Pottersfield Press has followed, reproducing her work as it appears in that book.

There Is Life Everywhere

The ever-moving leaves of a poplar tree lessened my anxiety as I walked through the woods trying to make my mind work on a particular task I was worried about. The ever-moving leaves I touched with care, all the while talking to the tree. "Help me," I said. There is no help from anywhere, the moving story I want to share. There is a belief that all trees, rocks, anything that grows is alive, helps us in a way that no man can ever perceive, let alone even imagine. I am a Mi'kmaw woman who has lived a long time and know which is true and not true – you only try if you do not believe – I did, that is why my belief is so convincing to myself. There was a time when I was a little girl, my mother and father had both died and [I was] living at yet another foster home which was far away from a native community. The nearest neighbours were non-native and their children never went near our house, though I went to their school and got along with everybody, they still did not go near our home. It was at this time I was so lonely and wanted to play with other children my age which was twelve at the time. I began to experience unusual happiness when I lay on the ground near a brook just a few metres from our yard. At first I lay listening to the water; it seemed to be speaking to me with a comforting tone, a lullaby at times. Finally I moved my playhouse near it to be sure I never missed the comfort from it. Then I developed a friendship with a tree near the brook. The tree was just there, I touched the outside bark, the leaves I did not tear but caressed. A comforting feeling spread over me like warmth, a feeling you cannot experience unless you believe. That belief came when I was saddest. The sadness did not return after I knew that comfortable unity I shared with all living animals, birds, even the well I drew the water from. I talked to every bird I saw, the trees received the most hugs. Even today, others do not know the unconditional freedom I have experienced from the knowledge of knowing that this is possible. Try it and see. There is life everywhere, treat it as it is, it will not let you down.

Imaginary Buddies

My dad dies in Millbrook Reservation, Nova Scotia, in 1942
I am ten years old, I hear the voices of an Indian Agent and others
They are discussing where to put me, finally a name I hear
Oh, not there. Just a few days ago I was in a group throwing rocks
At a man in the bushes. All the children did not like the man.
While I am thinking what to do next, somebody takes my hand
Leads me away, I follow with ease, knowing the person.
My next home place is Oxford Junction. With three native families
In September I go to school with non-natives, I try to make friends
The girls are friendly at school but not allowed to go to my home.
I ask why? No answer. The other natives live too far, no playmates.
My imaginary world begins, the maple my friend, the aspen my friend
The birds and every animal became my friend, in a while many
    friends.
I fed the birds and animals, hugged the trees, feeling good
And noticed that if you are good to anything, payback double
I even had names for my trees – Tom, John, Maria, like my sister
The big spruce was *Kujinu'* (Grandfather). The short balsam *Kijinu'*
Kujinu' and *Kijinu'* always smelled nice, so gentle, their arms touch.
And as long as I was at my playhouse I was happy.
When away sad.
My foster mother wondered why I was happy while alone at my
    playhouse
Her questions were not answered. One time I did, was called crazy
She inspected, nothing or nobody. Her look incredulous
To this day I like feeding birds and little animals
Once when I came home from the hospital, there were many birds
On telephone line all looking towards my house
Thank you, I told them. They still visit.

The Solid Part of One's Identity

In the expression of my tongue
I say, *Kesalin*? Do you love me?
I may say *Kesalu'l*, I love you.
Positive words are important
I do not teach hate
The solid part of one's identity
Is communication,
Exchanging words or touch
With no animosity towards another.
I have had positive experience
The past twenty-two years of writing
Trying to teach the Mi'kmaw way of life
The majority of Mi'kmaw are peace-keeping people
They are gentle people, anxious to please
I sympathize with my people across the nation
I admire what they think should be done
But do not think a militant attitude should be used
The solid part of our identity is sharing
That is why we are here today
We are survivors.

My Heroes Were the People I Knew

The best thing one can do is to believe in one's self
That is if there is no backup
The inner glow in one's heart
Which everyone of us have had at one time or other.
That as you know is *Niskam*
He has been my major backup since I started to write
Asking for help each time, using my own words.
Today the feeling is good because of past accomplishment
Something that was done
The feeling is like climbing a ladder of happiness.
You do not want it to end but it does
Is it enough for now until another burst of inspiration?
It is you who decides, either you fall on your face
Or be a winner.
Maybe then you can do something for the community
The nation as a whole, or even your loved ones.
It helps to do what one thinks best.
The goal I set for myself was, they are going to see a good Indian
I also represent a good nation, it took a lot of effort.
My heroes were the people I knew, the elders, the people my age
The children are number one, that realization is what keeps me
Going, until such time I cannot do it anymore. *Ta'ho'*

When I Am Gone

When I am gone, don't cry but smile and think;
Remember the car ride we had and talked about nothing
We said something about the trees, the hills behind our homes
The church we met on Sunday, *Pe'kwam-uk-sin*, we hugged
You walked by and you stopped, we had a little chat
Nothing important, maybe about our children
Or how to cook bannock that is crisp
We drank tea together, remembering the old days.
Oh yes we have a lot in common, our husbands gone
To work and communicate with their friends.
The long wait till payday, so you have discussions about
What we need for home, our ideas put together
Women for women, men for men and our children
Who always need something

Yes, my friend
We are all the same, just ask the next person
Did she die?
Then smile, because I'll be happy
At least you asked.

Catherine Martin

A member of the Millbrook First Nation in Truro, Nova Scotia, Catherine Martin is an independent producer, director, writer, facilitator, communications consultant, drummer, and the first woman Mi'kmaw filmmaker from the Atlantic region. She has a B.A. from Dalhousie University in Theatre Arts and a Masters of Education from Mount Saint Vincent with a focus on Media Literacy. She lives in Blind Bay, Nova Scotia, with her family.

Catherine's award-winning documentaries include the animation film *Little Boy Who Lived with Muini'skw* (2004), the NFB film *The Spirit of Annie Mae* (2002), and *Spirit Wind* (2000). In 2006, Catherine added the NFB online documentary *Bringing Annie Mae Home* to her many accomplishments.

Catherine is the past chairperson of the Board of Directors for Aboriginal Peoples Television Network (APTN), the first co-chair of Dalhousie University's Indigenous Black and Mi'kmaq Law Program, and the past chair of the Society for Canadian Artists of Native Ancestry. She has helped to develop many of the policies and programs within the Canadian cultural and arts institutions to advance First Nations artists in their respective disciplines and has advocated for educational access to professional careers. She was the interim director with Nations In A Circle, an Atlantic Aboriginal arts organization.

Catherine and her company have worked with several Mi'kmaq and Maliseet organizations to produce corporate promotional videos that help to tell the story of individual initiatives such as the Unamaki Economic Benefits Office and the Ulnooweg Development Group. She was a contributor to *Aboriginal Oral Traditions* (2008) and is a regular contributor to *Mi'kmaq-Maliseet Nations News*. She teaches Mi'kmaq and Aboriginal history and culture at universities and in communities across Canada and the U.S., including Cape Breton University. Catherine has been featured in recent documentaries and television shows such as APTN's *Storytellers In Motion* (2008).

Oral Tradition

As a Mi'kmaq filmmaker and storyteller I am always challenged with the absence of written, visual or other materials from the Mi'kmaq culture. The following essay was written for a publication titled *Aboriginal Oral Traditions* (2008), which explores the issues around the recovery of lost memory and effaced cultural history within one's culture. It is a subject near and dear to my heart, one that I struggle with and am challenged by others about. I have a firm belief that the story is within our living memories, in our connection to our ancestors, in our genes, in our blood, and in our spirit. The story is sacred and requires to be treated in a sacred, respectful manner by accepting the responsibility from within our communities to continue to tell the story from our place of knowing.

As the first Mi'kmaw First Nations filmmaker in the Atlantic region, I have come to this conclusion after making films by and about the Mi'kmaq community for over twenty years. I was raised within a Mi'kmaq family where stories were told to me all the time. I come from a wonderful tradition of storytellers who were basket makers, trappers, hunters, fishers and prospectors. I can speak from a perspective that people can only get if they are immersed within their culture.

This telling of the story as a way to begin a healing process is one of the most powerful methods I know to help begin a dialogue over what many have been silent about. The telling of a story from the perspective of those whose lives it impacted is vital to getting to the heart of the story, to the truth. I am committed to and take the position that our stories need to be told by our own people. This is not saying that our stories should not be told from an outside perspective. If they are, then it should be understood that the story is coming from an outside worldview, written, directed and edited from outside the perspective of the people it is about. To accomplish the telling of a story from the first-people perspective, it needs to be researched, written, directed, produced, and edited by those from within that culture in order for it to truly be told in the purest sense. It is difficult to accomplish this when we as First Nations, Inuit and Métis do not have the resources to ensure the process involves the very people the story is about.

It is my affirmation that the telling of our stories from a different place of knowing, from our view, our eyes, our hearts is important and necessary. I tell stories from a Mi'kmaq perspective. It is the place I am most comfortable in because it is the place I come from. Being Mi'kmaq is all that I am and will ever be. I was born Mi'kmaq and will die Mi'kmaq. The stories I tell, no matter what story, will always be from a Mi'kmaq perspective.

This all leads me to discussing my own work and why I chose to pursue a career in filmmaking, or more to the point, why it chose me. As I mentioned, I am a descendent of a storytelling tradition. I have been nurtured by storytelling, raised to understand life through stories and taught to remember them as they are told to me over and over again. I always knew the power of telling stories and especially those told from the heart, from the place of knowing, from the one who experienced it. When I went to elementary school I learned at a very young age what discrimination and racism is. I learned through reading stories, articles and books written about Aboriginal peoples throughout history and current issues. My eyes were opened wide to this cruel world where

Aboriginal people are not considered the proud, loving people I had grown up with. It was confusing as a young person to be told by those in authority, those who are your teachers, those who supposedly come from a place of knowing, that we are inferior. It was tough to listen to and was embarrassing at times to identify as a Mi'kmaq among those who were not.

I made it through those years and they were good lessons to learn. The experience made me a stronger person. It also helped me to mould my life in later years when the opportunity to make films was presented to me by the National Film Board's Atlantic Executive Producer at the time, Germaine Wong, and Mi'kmaq Association of Cultural Studies Director, Dr. Peter Christmas. In 1991, they asked me to direct a film, *Kwa'nu'te'*, on Mi'kmaq and Maliseet artists. I agreed to the challenge because I knew I could do this. I saw stories produced on my grandfather, Mike Martin, and on my dad, Ben Martin, and thought then I could have done that. In fact, I thought I could have done it better since I knew them and understand their world as a Mi'kmaq.

So I made my first film with the goal to learn how to make a great film and one day make the film I needed to make. I knew Annie Mae Pictou Aquash, the Nova Scotia-born Mi'kmaq activist who was a powerful woman in the American Indian Movement in the 1970s, had a story to tell and wasn't given the chance when she was murdered in 1975. She was silenced by someone who had no right to make judgment on another's right to life. I knew she wanted to tell a story and one day, I would help her tell that story. That has become my role as a storyteller who uses film as a medium to reach the audiences, to help others tell the story of the people.

I think that one of the most important experiences was just before I made *The Spirit of Annie Mae*. The Chief of Miawpukek First Nation, the only Mi'kmaq band in Newfoundland recognized by the government, approached me. Chief (Sagamaw) Mi'sel Joe told me about a vision he had of one day building a birchbark canoe and paddling it from Newfoundland to Nova Scotia. This journey would help to reunite the Mi'kmaq nation and to heal his community. The process of building a canoe from natural resources and paddling it would help them to reconnect to their ancestors and relearn the ancient ways of navigating by the stars. I asked if I could document the journey and he said he would allow it to be filmed since it would be important to the future generations.

In 1997, the chief contacted me to come and join them on their journey across the waters to Chapel Island, Nova Scotia, from Cape Ray, Newfoundland. They had built the canoe and were ready to sail. I scrambled to develop proposals to find the funding to finance this film project. I was deeply disappointed when I was turned down by the NFB Aboriginal program and other federal departments. It was such a disappointment I decided to do it anyway without any support except that from some good friends and some in-kind support from the Canadian Coast Guard and Aboriginal Affairs for Nova Scotia. During the process, Vision TV did commit to a broadcast license and in the third year The Canada Council offered me a grant from their mainstream funding after the Aboriginal Secretariat jury declined my application.

Basically, I produced, directed, shot and assistant-edited the entire film. It took three years to complete the journey and one year to edit. The experience gave me everything I needed to begin the making of *The Spirit of Annie Mae*. It was like boot camp for me. The story of *Spirit Wind* was told from a Mi'kmaq perspective, it was a Mi'kmaq journey and it was the realization of a Mi'kmaq chief's vision. It has empowered me to do so much more in my life and convinced me of the power of telling a story from our own perspective.

In 1999, during the making of *Spirit Wind*, I co-curated a photographic exhibit with two colleagues, Tim Bernard and Leah Rosenmeier, using photos of four Mi'kmaq communities taken in 1930 by American ethnographer Frederick Johnson. The result of the collaboration was a touring exhibit with a videotape of elders from the community who helped to tell the stories of the people in the photos. We also produced a book with the images and stories.

This experience further convinced me of the incredible resource that exists within our own people, the memory of our elders who carry within their living memory the collective memory of our nation. It was amazing to listen to the elders recall stories about grandparents, great-grandparents, many of whom they had never met or seen in a photo.

The affirmation that our stories, our oral histories, are still valid gave me so much faith and conviction in the telling of our stories from within our own truths, from our perspectives. The exhibit and the book, *Mikwite'imanej Mikmaqi'k: Let Us Remember the Old Mi'kmaq* (Nimbus, 2001), make me proud to have been part of such an important gift to the future. I had many experiences prior to the making of the film which gave me strength and courage to tackle the Annie Mae project. These experiences were all part of the teachings I needed in order to be prepared to tell Annie Mae's story. They have given me insight and led me to places I needed to go before I went on the road to find out about her.

I did make the film on Annie Màe Aquash with the National Film Board and completed it in 2004. Her story was told by those who knew her – her sisters, her ex-husband, her two daughters and the good friends she spent time with over her short life of thirty years. For the most part, the story was told from a female perspective, shedding light on a period in history that has mainly been told from a male point of view.

I have come to believe in this as a means to bring our stories into the future in a way that will not confuse our generations to come when they are searching for truths, for identity, for teachings. The stories told from our perspective will help to keep alive our culture, our language, our worldview. Up to this point, it has been very difficult to wade through the histories and stories told by outsiders and to search for the hidden messages in these histories sent to us by our ancestors. The impact of someone else's imposed value system on our own has destroyed many of our ways. The writing of our histories and our stories, as well as the interpretation of our songs and art, from outside perspectives has caused much confusion to those today who are searching for our own truths, our identity as a people.

The truths are within our collective memories. The identity we so desperately need in order to heal our communities after five hundred years can be found through the process of telling our own stories in our own way – through our own eyes and from our collective memories as a people. When we continue to allow those from outside our culture and our nations the privilege of telling our stories from their outside perspectives, we only do an injustice to our children and our future generations. The honourable and respectful thing to do for one who is in a position of power, of privilege, is to use that influence to ensure that who tells our stories, who gets financial support to produce films about ourselves, are those from within the place of knowing – those who possess the cultural capital, property and authority to tell the stories of their people. The time has come for those outside our culture to relinquish control and allow the storytellers to reclaim their rightful place in society. For too long, the impact of Eurocentric values and culture has spread over our way of life like blankets infested with smallpox. Let the storytellers take back their original place of honour and privilege. The story is sacred.

Jean Augustine-McIsaac

Jean Augustine-McIsaac was born in Elsipogtog, New Brunswick, but later came to Nova Scotia and always lived close to Kejimkujik. She was very knowledgeable about her Mi'kmaw heritage and traditions, and was an acknowledged spiritual leader. She worked at Kejimkujik National Park, where she headed the Cultural Interpretation section and worked hard to preserve and properly present the history of the Mi'kmaq. In 2003, she designed the commemorative monument at Kejimkujik, saying that it was "for all the Mi'kmaw People. Let it be a reminder of the past, healing for the present, and a promise for the future." She also hosted an annual mawiomi (gathering) in Kejimkujik and passed on traditional teachings to all who wished to learn. Jean passed in 2011, and is keenly missed.

As a member of the Bear clan, Jean honoured Muin by conducting Bear Feast ceremonies twice a year, in the spring and fall. One year, as she began to explain the significance of the Bear Feast, the spirits gave her the following story in its entirety.

How Muin Became Keeper of the Medicines

In the beginning of time, people lived in harmony with the land. They lived in harmony with their brothers and sisters, the plants, trees, animals, insects, snakes, the fish and the birds. The people realized that the plants and animals were of spirit, and were placed here on Mother Earth to help them. The people were grateful for the help of the animals, the plants, and the trees and for that they wanted to honour them. One day they heard a beautiful song from a bird, and they became aware how this tiny creature made them feel. They wanted to sing in return, to make the spirit of the animals feel as they did when they heard the songs of the birds. And so they asked for songs from the spirits to sing to their brothers and sisters, the animals, plants, and fish. Songs came to the people: songs to be sung to the spirit of the eagle, the spirit of the tree, the spirit of the water – songs for all of their relations.

One day Muin was in the forest and he heard one of these songs being sung by the people. The song was being sung in his honour, and their voices were carried by the wind into the forest. When Muin heard this beautiful song he felt honoured and respected. He went to the edge of a clearing in the forest, and saw that the people were in ceremony. As he watched and listened, he saw the people making offerings to his spirit, and he heard the kind words that the people spoke of him. They referred to him as

Brother. Then he heard the people ask him for medicines to help them.

At that moment, Muin realized that he must make a journey for the people and bring back medicines for them. All summer long he ate and ate, preparing for his task. At last, when fall came, he knew it was time. He sought out a lodge where his physical form would be safe while his spirit travelled. As he approached his lodge he looked back on the world, as he knew he would be gone for several moons. Finally, with the words "All my relations," he entered his lodge.

And so the spirit of Muin began its quest into the spirit world. As he journeyed, he collected the medicines the people had asked for. He sat in council with the spirits of the plants and requested from them the medicines for the people. The plants agreed to give their medicines, as long as Muin would cultivate and fertilize the land for them, so they would continue to come back year after year. Muin agreed to do this.

Finally, after many moons, Muin's journey was coming to an end. He wanted to let the people know he would soon be returning, so his spirit found a woman of the Bear Clan, who was praying in the sweat lodge. Muin came to that woman and spoke to her: "From this day forward, you will be known as Muiniskw, the Bear Woman. I have a request for you. I am soon returning to my physical form, as I have completed my spirit journey. Would you be so kind as to prepare a feast for me, as I am weak."

The woman knew that when a spirit requested something from a human it was to be done. Muiniskw listened to Muin's request as to how the feast would be prepared and what ceremonies would be involved. Then she took the request to the people. She told them of her vision in the lodge, and shared with the people the details of Muin's request. The people were happy and immediately began preparations for the feast. Muiniskw told of the berries that Muin asked for. She said that Muin wanted the berries he feasted on throughout the year, and he wanted to honour the spirit of the plants that provided him with this food, as they also provided the food for the people.

And so it was. People brought berries, which were dried and stored over the winter: strawberries, which were the first berry in the spring; blueberries, fruit of summer; blackberries from the fall; and cranberries gathered in early winter. Then the men went out to their weirs and gathered fish to be included in the feast.

Four days after the Bear Spirit spoke to Muiniskw the appointed day for the Feast for the Bear arrived. The berries and the fish were all prepared by Muiniskw, and more food was prepared by the women. As the people sat in a Sacred Circle, the ceremony began with the lighting of the Sacred Pipe, and as the pipe was shared with the people a story was told. The story told of why we must always honour the Bear Spirit. In the fall of the year we honour him for his long fast, and the journey he is about to make into the spirit world for medicines for the people. In the spring we honour the Bear for the medicines he brings back from his long journey. In both ceremonies a woman of the Bear Clan prepares the Feast for the Bear, and in both ceremonies the people sing a song to honour Muin.

And so it continues to this day. Muin tills and fertilizes the ground to help plants grow, and during the long cold winter he journeys to the spirit realm to seek medicines for the people. And each year, in the fall and the spring, Native people gather together for a feast in his honour.

Alice Azure

Alice Azure's writings have appeared in a number of journals and anthologies such as *The Florida Review*; *Native Literatures: Generations*; *Yellow Medicine Review*; *Whisper n Thunder*; *I Was Indian: An Anthology of Native Literature*; *Visions and Voices: American Indian Activism and the Civil Rights Movement*; *Many Mountains Moving*; *Yukhika-latuhse*; *Mid Rivers Review*; and *Birthed from Scorched Hearts: Women Respond to War*. The St. Louis Poetry Center, to which she belongs, published her prize-winning poems in its annual chapbooks of 2007 and 2008. Albatross Press released her first book, *In Mi'kmaq Country: Selected Poems & Stories*, in 2007. Her most recent books (2011) are a memoir, *Along Came a Spider* from Bowman Books, and a chapbook of poems, *Games of Transformation*, published by Albatross Press.

A Mi'kmaq Métis whose roots are in the Kespu'kwitk District of Nova Scotia, Alice grew up in a children's home in Cromwell, Connecticut. She earned an M.A. degree in urban and regional planning from the University of Iowa. Retiring in 2005 as vice-president of services and planning for the United Way of Southeastern Connecticut, she then moved to Maryville, Illinois, to be close to her four grandchildren.

Unknown

A friend entrusts
this skirt to me,
its black threadbare wool
held to calico backing
by stitches through
thousands of beads
arranged ankle to waist –
two silver vines
full of bright flowers
crimson on mauve
yellow opaque –
each rooted within
an array of leaves
along the hemline row.

Nothing is known
of this dancing skirt
found at some eastern sale –
tribe, place and artist
not indicated –
provenance silent
like my grandmothers' names –

unknown by priests
no matter the rite –
birth, marriage, death –
recorded as *inconnu*,
arbitrarily labelled
Marie or *Amerindienne*
until thousands grace
our genealogies.

Will the skirt's creator
keep step with me –
dance when I dance –
my body a blooming trellis
for her dazzling flowers?
Will my *Marie Amerindienne*
know I sprouted from a seed
that fell and flourished
from her family tree?

Elegy from Matanzas Pass
(Fort Meyers Beach, Florida)

Consider Macondo's[1] children –
fungicide, insecticide,
household cleaner,
ink and rubber flippers.

Her children are legion –
highway, dashboard,
polyester zipper,
elastic and plastic.

Demand unending
for her offspring,
the rig squats mindlessly –
drills down with blades

that cut through pipes –
marauds her gulf-sized womb
until the black-gold blood
explodes from her deep –

spews tar-ball clots
into pristine waters, gums
the grassy nests of terns,
gulls, plovers and pelicans.

Oh God of the universe,
have mercy upon
Macondo's hemorrhage –
livelihoods lost to a poisoned Gulf.

---

1 The oil that spilled into the Gulf of Mexico from April to July of 2010 came from a reservoir called the Macondo Prospect, located under 5,000 feet of water and 13,000 feet of rock.

From King Philip's Seat
(Bristol, Rhode Island)

At the Haffenreffer Museum, I listened
to Marge's lecture about New England's
ethnobotany, and how Native Americans used
common plants for medicine, food, shelter, and decoration –
for ceremonies incurring good thoughts.

She must have cast a spell that day
the way she talked about the little
sunflowers that grow on nine-foot stalks,
sprout gnarled tubers that look like fresh ginger,
and taste delicious roasted on an open fire.
My eyes fastened upon her several slides
of gold-yellow fields loaded with full-blossomed
Jerusalem artichokes. In an off-handed way
lost to the audience, but not to me, she said,
"Where they grow like that,
you can be sure Indians lived there."

Determined to have these Native beauties
adorn my garden, I asked my sister
from Woodstock, Connecticut –
once a praying Indian town –
to dig some clumps for me.

Now, in late summer, bouquets
of sunchokes grace my kitchen table
and the graves of warrior relatives
at Rock Island National Cemetery.
When I travel in early autumn,
I smile at all the roadside spots
where ubiquitous yellow suns
bask on top of sturdy stems
heralding Indian Country.

A Blessing

To posts and crossbeams of her cedar arbor
I secured my web, silvery spokes and lines
reflecting full moonlight. I can hardly wait
to hear her happy *Hello*! – surprise in seeing me
tonight. For her I build my house in clear sight,
concrete places – tops of computer pages or
between tall stems of goldenrod and mustard weed –
no dreams or visions with their layered meanings.

My best surprise was at an outdoor Mass to bless
the church's animals. I – a deity –
and leader of the Spider Clan, made a grand
emergence through the turf in front of where she sat.
Her eyes agog, wet in wonder, she knew I
came – not to claim – but to bestow ancient blessings.

Mixing Bowl

His clerical collar damp with sweat
moved my mother – Lutheran-bred –
to invite the Black man in.
The warmth of his eyes and smile of his face
radiated rare kindness
around our rough space.
She brought out her mixing bowl
filled with cool water
he poured on my head.
Praying quiet words,
he dedicated my young life
to the Son of Light.

Decades later, moorings lost,
I asked for help from healer friends.
They smudged and smoked
to woodland spirits, prayed
for my renewal.

When the songs were over,
I rested upon the ground,
watched a spider labour along a blade of grass,
bowl of embers balanced on her back.

Later, I knew Old Grandmother –
who long ago brought Sun's fire to the People –
had poured her light into my soul.

Family Callout

Today a daughter phones me that she's homeless.
It seems her landlord, like the cops, believes
she hosts a house of drugs. She can't perceive
the harm that's done by her children's friends, who roam
around her home, devour her meagre store
of food, self-confidently ply their XTC-driven
civility. I offer advice, guilt-ridden
about how little I help. Oh, how I deplore
the prison of poverty!
                              Again, a callout begins
of cousins, aunties, uncles and parents who found
their paths. These teachers, warriors and ranchers expound
upon the importance of skills. A family sit-in
commences. We pray and sing nightlong,
dreaming lost memories reborn, like a cradlesong.

HOMELANDS
(Geneseo, Illinois)

After the Christmas storm, my daughter's husband
plowed some paths around their place
allowing easier access into the woods.
I watch my grandchildren frolic along the tracks,
disappear down the hill. How long
has it been since I wandered in trees and brush
mindless of poison ivy, muck or getting lost?
Come on, says David, *I'll show you around*.

He drives his half-ton pickup to the edge
of the ravine. Down we go, I stepping
into his footprints as he points out oak, cherry and ash –
patches where pink and white trillium will bloom.
Along a rippling stream, we follow deer tracks
to a spot where David stops and quietly motions
to the other side – up the hill a ways. A conical mound
nestles in the hollow's side. *There's another
nearby*, he says. *I'll drive you there*.

We drive out to Angel Ferry Road, cut across
a neighbour's field, turn right and begin the approach
to where the mound lay reposed.
David adjusts the gears to make a turn
around the mound. Back wheels slip, churn
snow and dirt into the air. I cringe at how
this noise disrupts hallowed ground,
once homeland to Mesquawkie and Sauk.
Mitakuye Oyasi, I whisper. *All My Relations*.

Resigned to being stuck, we turn, face knee-deep
snow and the mile-long hike back to his house.
My footsteps trace his. I am not winded
nor does anything ache. *It's the endorphins*,
my daughter says, once I'm inside her house.
Perhaps. I wonder about the day's strange gift
of energy visited upon my body, and remind
my son-in-law to lay sweet grass by the mounds.

"Mixing Bowl" and "Unknown" appeared in *In Mi'kmaq Country: Selected Poems & Stories* (Albatross Press, 2007). "A Blessing" was first published in the e-journal *Native Literatures: Generations*, Volume 1, Number 1 (July 2010) and later in the memoir *Along Came A Spider* (Bowman Books, 2011). "Family Callout" was first included in *Moving Many Mountains* Volume IX, Number 1 (2008-09) and subsequently in the poetry chapbook *Games of Transformation* (Albatross Press, 2011). "Elegy from Matanzas Pass" was previously published in *Native Literatures: Generations*, Volume 1, Number 3 (October 2010).

Denise Larocque

Born in the U.S.A., Denise is originally from the community of Gesgapegiag, Quebec, where she played an important role in implementing the first traditional powwow in 1993. She is a Pipe Carrier and a Spirit Walker who enjoys blogging and writing.

An activist for women's issues, Denise was the winner of The Denise Briére Award 2006-2007 for helping the most women in her regional county municipality. Additionally, she was a finalist for the Quebec government's Le Prix Égalité in 2008, nominated for her organization of *The Vagina Monologues* for English, French, and Mi'kmaq women for the Prevention de la Violence event. She has been a contributing writer for *Migmawei Gespisiq Magazine* and in May 2007 won third place for Best Column from the Quebec Community Newspaper Association. Currently, she is working on a pilot project by the Quebec Native Women on Healthy Sexuality, creating women's wellness retreats, and pursuing traditional Mi'kmaq midwifery. Denise is the proud mother of four.

Walking Straight – Tepag'peniei

The story of the spirit walk has been one of the hardest things I have ever tried to write, I think in part because the story itself has a spirit of its own, the kind of story that needs to be shared orally, as our ancestors once did. I say that because it's been well over a decade that I have been trying to write the story of the spirit walk, and yet the words never seem to come freely. Even in the eighteen years since the walk first began, I would say that I have only told it a handful of times. Each time I tell it, it has no order, no start nor finish. What comes out always seems to be exactly what the listener needed to hear. I can give the details of the stories – the who, what, when, where and why – but in all honesty eighteen years ago is a long time, and although there are parts of the story etched in my mind forever, I fear that I may not do it justice. Another amusing point is the fact that other spirit walkers, months after the walk, recalled details that did not match mine. Some would say, "We walked sixteen days" where I counted fourteen or "We walked 360 miles" as opposed to my 280. Who's right and who's wrong is not the point. The point is that the story is in the words of the teller, so even if you meet a spirit walker in your path after my version reaches you, just know that this is how I remembered it ...

The walk itself was first given to a man who lived in Maine. Known as Lone Bear, as a child he played on a mountain near his parents' home, and played with the spirits of the mountain. As most children do, as they grow they seem to lose that sense of imagination along with the lack of parental support of that imagination. This happened to the boy and the spirits no longer presented themselves to him. One day, many, many years after his childhood adventures, he found himself in a place in life where he needed guidance. He remembered his time spent on Lone Bear Mountain and climbed it for answers. What weighed heavy on his heart was the intense negative connection between white and Native people. The spirits guided him and spoke to him once again. They told him about a silent spiritual walk that would help bring peace between the two nations, "a walk for unity." The walk would start on top of that very mountain and would end in Big Cove, New Brunswick. It was also an opportunity to walk and pray for young Mi'kmaq people whose lives were being taken in large numbers by a serpent that got stronger in the sky with every life deliberately taken.

Lone Bear was assured that the people from those two nations would come to walk. Over several meetings on the mountain, Lone Bear was told many things including instructions to get the word out. The spirits requested that walkers leave their sacred objects at home, dress as if they were just out for a walk, walk in silence, walk in a straight line, bring only three days food ration, and walk with our faith in the Creator. When news of the walk finally reached me, I was told that it was a ten-day silent walk, and that there were those who were meant to walk and those who would help. I was not certain which category I fell into – I just knew that without a doubt I had to go. I bought myself a new pair of sneakers and started to walk, going a bit further each day until I could walk five kilometres. Then I would rest a week in pain and then walk again.

My journey started out from Gesgapegiag, Quebec, also known as Mala or Maria. Even though we were asked to leave our spiritual items at home, I still felt the need for protection, so I packed my walking stick with hawks' feathers that broke en route and my medicine bag that I swear was stolen on the mountaintop by the Geow-lud-mo-sis-eg (The Little People). If memory serves me correctly, we were six from my community, two from Listuguj and a white witch from Campbelton, New Brunswick. Really, a real witch! We headed to Eel Ground where my elder and his sons lived, the ones who first told me about the walk. A sweat lodge was scheduled before we set out to Mapleton, Maine, to the mountain where the walk would begin. That sweat in the turtle lodge was very powerful for me. I remember seeing in the dark everyone's spirit. We looked like a bunch of white ghosts, but the thing I remember most was that none of us were male or female – we were just spiritual beings encompassed by a body that gave us that title of being male or female.

It's strange to me how trusting I was. We didn't know the fellow who led us, someone named David, yet we followed him down a never-ending railroad track, into a forest, over a river where the running joke was that the "Newfie fell in" (started by the Newfoundlander himself), sleeping bag and all. Or was it just the sleeping bag? It did occur to me halfway up the mountain that I did not know this guy and yet felt safe in his presence – that is, of course, after the thoughts of axes and strange Kool-Aid passed through my mind. Years later I heard that the running joke on us walkers was that we were followers of this guy, as if in some cult. I wondered if perhaps his having the given name David had something to do with it.

Before the walk we were informed that we only needed three days supply of food and that the Creator would provide everything we needed after that. Walking up that mountain without any water I remember the apple juice never quite quenched my thirst. David told us of a spot were the water came straight out of the ground and fresh from the mountain. I shared my juice only out of pure selfishness, waiting for the Creator to lead me to water. Incidentally, I never found my water until the next day and we ended up melting snow, dirt and all. I learned that water is important. When we finally reached the top many people were exhausted. We witnessed a hurt knee healed by Lone Bear, although he said it was the spirit of the injured woman's grandfather, not him. She looked very surprised when he mentioned that her grandfather was a carpenter, because as it turned out he was. Some people en route saw spirits while others, including me, did not.

Once I reached the top I looked over the side, closest to the cliff, at the most spectacular view, and with tear-filled eyes my first thought was "I am home." The fear came back as David informed us he was leaving us up on the mountain while he proceeded to (in my mind, sleep in the comforts of his own home) head down to wait for more people. Many of us learned an important lesson that day: that food, shelter, water and warmth are far more important than any material things.

We spent the next few days on the mountain, playing, exploring, learning, sharing and laughing. We learned that when we offered a spirit plate to the night sky, it lit up with thunder beams as if the spirits were saying, "Thank you!" I started to notice in those three days a strange event was unfolding. In the beginning, the white people were on one side of our newly furbished community kitchen, which was located around the firepit, while the Natives seemed to be hanging together around their side. We all made a group decision to share our food since our supply was low, but some of us were reluctant, including me. Many of us did not bring enough for three days, while others left theirs in cars, thinking they could just run back for it after setting up camp. Food was prepared and shared sparingly the first night. I shared my stock but my survival instincts kicked in, making me hide some crackers in my tent. My rationalization behind doing so was "After all, I'm not going to starve."

On the morning of day two, the food supply was slim. By lunch I noticed that the non-Natives ate healthier than we did, us with our cans of Chef Boyardee and them with their dried nuts, berries, fresh fruits and vegetables with a few handfuls of couscous thrown in. I remember thinking my canned food did not look so yummy. There was a big part of me that was uncomfortable with the "them and us" division that seemed so apparent. I did, however, notice the Mi'kmaq people were open and sharing freely as if we were all family, while the white people were nervous to come and take a share of the food and tea. It made me see how our people have always been sharing and treated each other as family. I, being half and half of both nations, took it upon myself to use the Native hospitality I had learned at powwows to offer some tea to one of the ladies. Things seemed to warm up with the two nations as the day went on; people talked more, laughed more, sang and with the arrival of more food feasted together all day since we were to start the walk the next day with no food. Sharing was my second teaching as I stopped hoarding my crackers.

During my exploration on the mountain, I received a teaching while picking up a beautiful rock that shimmered with crystals on it. As I picked it up, I heard with surprise in my mind, in my own voice, a teaching: "Life is like a game, and like in video games, there are always ways to gain energy to get a longer life. In life we also get energy. Learn to fill your energy in a good and positive way because stealing energy loses you points." The teaching went on about the greed and rape of the earth's resources, that the taking of these resources represented materialistic things and selfishness, while the energy represented God and life itself. The lesson is about making decisions that help others and everything around us.

It was the day after the eclipse of the sun and we prepared for our walk down the mountain after three days of play and relaxation, which left our spirits high. Before the sun rose we had parting words and learned that we were walking with 100,000 spirits, some of which were our relatives. We were also told that they started to walk before us, and that this walk was done thousands of years before. As we headed down the mountain in silence, my mind was filled with thoughts. At one point I realized the hilarious way in which we packed our clothes and sleeping bags. Some stuffed them in green garbage bags tossed haphazardly over shoulders. We had our can openers, large bags of trash, and I was wearing my three-dollar antique backpack with its metal frame digging into my back. With my heavy cast iron pan clunking alongside, I thought, "We are no longer the people of the woods we once were."

On our way down, many of us tripped; we fell, helped each other up and down, and shed tears over clear-cutting. When we finally reached the bottom there was that sense of *we*, not *them and us*, not just *I* but a real sense of *we*. It was obvious that the journey was just about to begin. We would walk until the day after the eclipse of the moon. We were a large group of about twenty-five, walking towards the Canadian border. As I walked I learned in the silence of my mind that we walk in silence because words are sharp; it's the sharpness of the words that causes pain. In silence, we cannot lash out and blame others; we can only look within, and work on self. I remember praying for this one spirit walker to stop the way she was acting, bossing everyone around even in the silence, with a glare, a turn of her head, and a shake of her hand correcting our line. It started to bother me so I decided to pray, and my prayer went something like this: "Creator, can you make her stop bossing everyone around?" I heard, "No, you cannot ask others to change. You can only pray and ask that you are able to accept others for the way they are." It was a profound teaching for me.

Throughout that walk we learned that unconditional love is the key. As we stopped to rest in a parking lot, I recall feeling so drained and it was only the first day! We walked a total of twenty-five miles that day, counting the hike down the mountain with our gear. Luckily for us, the gear was now in tow in one of the vehicles that followed behind. Yet even without the gear I was exhausted. I had this feeling to stop, look down and pick up the reddest rock I had ever seen. I was told to ask it for energy and so I did. I felt energy, tingling going up into every fibre of my being. I heard the teaching, "The Creator is everywhere and in everything. If you need anything at all, all you need to do is ask." Which was probably a mistake on the spirits' part, telling us we could have anything we wanted, because we ended up asking for some things that were not contributing to our health, like chips, pop, and candy bars. Later I found out that many of us were also wishing for crabmeat, clam chowder, warm dry socks, raincoats, a warm place to sleep, and new sneakers. We got it all.

It was amazing the things that appeared everyday. Cars would stop and the occupants would say, "Hey, this is from the radio station, warm clam chowder and milk." (My silent request.) Then after a few hours a woman pulled up from a nearby Maliseet community and opened her trunk filled with hot traditional foods. I think we ate four meals that day. As we walked over the next couple of weeks the generosity was immense. People invited us into their homes, sheds and garages, fed us, offered tea, coffee and cookies. People would run up to hand us money and say, "This is everything I have." Churches opened their doors so we could sleep and get dry. Schools opened their bathrooms so we could wash. One town opened its armoury for us. As we walked in, everything you could want was there: healthy food, junk food and normal food. Stores donated pop, chips, chocolate bars, socks and raincoats. People came and did our laundry. After that we learned not to pray for things that would not assist our bodies for the long journey they would be continuing to carry us on.

As we walked the Renous Highway, I saw garbage of all sorts, from small non-biodegradable diapers to large refrigerators, bikes, and a television – garbage just dumped chaotically. There were lakes filled with black oil. Tears fell as I spent hours picking up the trash to no avail.

I learned as the days went on that we needed to take time and fill up our energy each day, and just as I asked that rock for some energy on the first day, I noticed that others found it in the hugging of trees, sitting on large boulders, putting their feet and hands in water, or walking into a forest. The spirit said, "It is up to you to find where your energy lies."

Through that walk, many mystical things happened. Eagles soared overhead each day, three deer followed us running out of the forest in the mornings, walking a ways with us and then showing up the next day for a total of four days. Horses seemed to stare into our souls and then danced in our presence as if knowing what we were doing. Black and white wolves appeared. I felt we were truly blessed and had an immense feeling that we were taking part in something truly amazing. We could hear our ancestors singing. We became somewhat telepathic, and I could see the white glow that surrounded us. A member in one of the towns later mentioned that it was as if we were floating on air, and honestly at times I felt that I was. Some walkers later said they felt as though they were being carried.

Throughout the walk we were told that one thousand people would walk with us, but every day I grew discouraged wondering when all these people would join us. It wasn't until the last five miles that the pain became immense; it was the most difficult stretch, yet also the most rewarding. Difficult because many walkers felt so heavy. Our blistered feet would carry us no more, and some walkers had to be carried over the five-mile mark. Rewarding because as we made our way into the community of Big Cove, now known as Elsipogtog, busload after busload joined our line of spirit walkers. The line grew so long that I could no longer see the front. And even though it was the most rewarding moment, it still brought tears of sadness to my eyes. I watched the youth, our future generations, walk in front of me tossing their garbage on Mother Earth. Flashbacks of the Renous came to mind and while they tossed what was left of their snacks on the ground, tears fell from my eyes as I recalled the past two weeks, how we always shared with one another, everything we had. What I learned in all that was the importance of sharing what you have with others, to take care of the Earth, to love and accept one another, and to practise unconditional love. At the end of the walk we had so much food and so many items to give away and to think we started with nothing. We were told that the Creator would provide and that He did.

Each year after that first walk, during the winter months, the spirit walkers would gather, new and old, to find out where and when the next walk would take place. It was through our dreams and visions throughout the year that we would piece together the next walk. Just before spring I found myself craving cool air in the nights and would leave my bedroom window open in preparation, yet yearn to go out on the lawn and sleep. I found myself craving dirt and wanting to eat with groups of silent friends. When spring arrived we gathered our items to walk in silence, each year becoming more and more the clever outdoorsmen, with better gear, warmer equipment, healthier food choices, yet with just as much garbage! With each walk I would grow excited knowing I would soon get to see Mother Earth awakening from her winter's sleep, see the buds on the trees slowly opening each day, and each day I walked I knew that I too would grow.

During the seven years of the spirit walks (from 1994 to 2000), I felt an evolution not only in myself but in others as well. Some of the most profound teachings I carry with me today were learned on those walks and are now part of the core values I live by. I chose the title "Walking Straight" because it took us years to learn to walk straight; we were told that by walking in a straight line like an arrow we would be stronger together. Through those seven years we walked in the seven Mi'kmaq districts: Kespukwitk, Sikepnékatik, Eskíkewaq, Unamákik, Piktuk aqq Epekwitk, Sikniktewaq, and Kespékewaq. With each walk I learned life's lessons, taught to me by the trees, earth, rocks, water, wind and animals.

The teachings would come in the silence of the mind, and it was through quieting the mind that you could hear the teachings which were hidden all around. If you listened carefully the elements would reveal their hidden teachings. I learned from the waters in Nova Scotia that each person has the ability to heal him- or herself. If we learn to use the sounds around us – the water crashing on the shores, the bubbling brooks, the birds chirping, the frogs croaking – they are all here to help to us heal. As I walked across Prince Edward Island, I learned of the power of dreams and spirits who were stuck. When I asked a snake who innocently passed by what he had to teach me, he said, "You need to learn to silence the mind, learn to be silent, for it is in the silence the teachings lie." As I walked, the rain said, "You need to learn to be in the present moment, to feel the droplets as they cleanse your skin, not to think about the past or dwell in the future, to just be." In Nova Scotia the wind said, "We have many ceremonies, but the most important ceremony is life itself, and the most important part of the ceremony is how we treat each other." For example, if we go to church, or our Native sweat lodge ceremony only to leave to gossip and hurt others with our words, we have just erased all the good we did in going to that ceremony.

This spirit walk was a seven-year journey that led us through the seven Mi'kmaq districts. Spirit walkers came and went with each passing year; some returned, yet others went their own way. You received the title of spirit walker if you walked ten minutes or ten miles, one walk or all seven. We all walked for many of our own reasons. Some walked for their children's children, while others walked for unity, for their people. Some walked for a better understanding, unconditional love or compassion. Most who participated felt moved to walk for some reason or another.

For some it was a positive experience and for others it was not. But most importantly it was a journey that took you within yourself. This spiritual silent walk taught you to be in the present moment: to work on self. To walk straight everyday is to be present, to walk with a compassionate heart, to silence the mind, to fill your energy in a good and positive way, and to place importance on family. When I think of the spirit walk, just the words spirit walk evoke in me everything I am. For several years this story has sat in my head and heart. Now its time has come to be shared. The spirit walker story belongs to all those who have walked, all those whose lives were touched by our presence, and now it belongs to you. "In spirit we walk!"

Charles Doucette

Charles Doucette of Chapel Island (Potlotek), Nova Scotia, is a visual artist who works in multiple media: he is engaged in painting, sculpture, photography, jewellery and other forms of art, including poetry. He makes use of everyday objects in his work, creating *Medallion* from an old tire and *Legend* using a photocopier. Of his exhibit *Legend*, which depicts increasingly faint images, at the Glooscap Heritage Centre and Mi'kmaq Museum in August 2010, he said, "I had the idea that I wanted to make art with a photocopier. Everything is digital now and it gets copied and recopied. The idea of 'Legend' is about how stories are told and retold and eventually details of the original start to fade."

Charles believes that writing down stories helps preserve them, but only through retelling from another storyteller can one get the feeling of time travel, that an actual portal through time has been opened. Charles's work can be seen at the Art Gallery of Nova Scotia and the Mount Saint Vincent University Gallery, both located in Halifax, and the Indian Art Centre in Ottawa. Visitors to Fortress Louisbourg National Historic Park can view the eight-pointed granite star Charles sculpted for the lookoff on the Mi'kmaw Trail. In 2010, he was one of seven Mi'kmaq artists chosen by the Vancouver 2010 Olympic Games for the Aboriginal Art Program;

works by over ninety Aboriginal artists decorated the Winter Games venues.

Charles is married to Lynne (Hatherill) Doucette of Kidderminster, England, and has four children, ranging in age from fifteen to twenty-two. In March 2011, Charles became a grandfather, when his granddaughter was born. Outside of art, Charles has had many occupations, including stints as a barge operator, a game warden, and an actor. Currently, he works seasonally as an Aboriginal Fishery Guardian. He is an avid hiker and kayaker.

Starlight
(The Boy Who Wouldn't Sleep)

A long time ago, a little boy didn't want to go to sleep. His mother, his father, and his grandmother told him, "Neap" (go to sleep). He wouldn't listen. One by one they fell asleep – first his grandmother, then his mother and finally his father.

The boy arose and played by the fire for a little while. Bored, he pushed back the wigwam entrance blanket and looked outside. Slowly, as his eyes adjusted to the dark, the boy saw something that amazed him. The sky was filled with stars, so many he could not count them all. They were so beautiful he began to cry, louder and louder until his crying woke his father. Waking up and finding his son missing, the father rushed outside. When he saw his son looking up and crying, he asked, "What's wrong? Did something hurt you?"

"No," said the boy. "I want them!"

"What?" said his father, pointing to the sky. "Those? You can't have those. They are the stars, and they are the spirits of our ancestors."

The boy began to cry again. His mother, awakened by the sound of talking and crying, came outside. "Dadagen kwis?" ("What's the matter, son?")

The boy sulked and protested, pointing to the sky. "I want them! But Dad says I can't have them!"

Wiping the tears from his eyes, his mother said, "Your dad's right – you can't have them."

Again the boy wept, louder and louder, stamping his feet, shouting, "I want them! I want them! I want them!"

This time the noise and commotion took Grandma away from her beautiful dream world. Slowly she rose. Her old bones creaking, she carried her blanket outside the wigwam to where the boy and his parents were standing. She put her arms and the blanket around the child, saying, "Na na dadagen kwis?" ("There, there. What's the matter, grandson?")

Wiping his tears, he told her how he had come to see this marvellous sight, so beautiful, so magical. He wanted the stars and when he asked her if he could have some of them, his grandmother, to his parents' bewilderment, said, "E'e." ("Yes.")

The parents asked, "How?"

The grandmother told her son-in-law, "Climb up the hill. When you get to the top, climb the tallest tree as high as you can. When you get to the top, close your eyes and reach up as far as you can. Close your hand and you will have captured a star. Apologize and thank the sky for the gift. Then open your eyes, climb down the tree, come back down the hill and back to the wigwam, holding the star tightly in your hand."

The son-in-law, knowing of the old woman's powers and being a good boy himself, obeyed her and did as she said. In his excitement coming back, feeling the warmth and seeing the glow in his hand, he began to run. But, just before he got back to the wigwam, he tripped over a tree root and let go of the star, smashing it to bits on a rock.

Some of the bits floated into the air and became the fireflies we see at night. The other bits became the crystals we see in the rocks by day. Today every little child can play with the stars of long ago each summer.

And it was also how the boy Starlight got his name.

Eva Apukjij

Eva Apukjij is a proud Wabanaki woman, mother and wife, from the Eastern door of Turtle Island, from the traditional territory of Oonamaki, the land of the mist and fog, better known as Cape Breton Island, Nova Scotia. She and her family settled in the community of We'koqma'q, the head of the waters, located in the foothills of Skye Mountain and on the shores of the Bras d'Or Lakes. This is where Eva was raised and she will forever be connected with the lands, waters, rivers and community. Eva and her husband Troy Gould have four sons, teenagers Blake and Wowkwis, Troy Jij, and Kaktogowaas and a daughter, Summer Rainbow.

Eva enjoys living and learning about the heritage of her people, who are constantly learning more about their history and dispelling old myths and lies. Their pride is deep-rooted and Eva likes learning new crafts and arts, writing, gardening, studying permaculture principles and design, canoeing, kayaking, nature walks and most of all, repatriating L'nu ways. Original ways are simple ways of life that are respectful and honour natural laws.

For the last four years, Eva has volunteered within her community and been a key player in starting and promoting a community gardening group, which feeds over seventy families healthy, nutritional foods. The group promotes the sacred three sisters of gardening – corn, squash and beans – and encourages the use and harvesting of wild natural foods that feed the mind, body and spirit well. These include fiddleheads, chanterelles, various wild berries, food obtained through fishing and hunting, and the use of ancient medicines. In this way, the garden group does its part in minimizing the environmental impact and supporting the great web of life.

Mu'skunimikpitek (The Colour Purple)

My heart aches in loneliness
Blank, numb and emotionless
Neither happy nor sad
Neither angry nor mad
A kind of limbo, where I stand
Empty, somewhat hollow
Give me peace, hope and balance
Forgiveness may mean giving
Happiness a chance
For so long have we been fighting
For treaty and understanding
Peace and friendship
Was always our intent
Ironically
This mission found us
In the midst of an ancient war instead
The heart can be so tricky
Raging fires sacred
Blowing the perfect storms
Winds of all directions,
Blow away and cleanse
The evil and wickedness
Where there is darkness,
Shine upon us and
Embrace the lights
Crying rivers,
Until clear and pristine
Letting go the pains
Until none remain
Water is the blood
Of our Mother Earth
Bleeding for all Creation
Through the devastation

Of our natural world
Help us find
Where the forgiveness is
How deep do we have to go?
We want to grow
Proceed
Feel beyond the sorrows
Spark peace, hope and balance
For the children of tomorrow

Wishing upon the falling stars
From the lights within our hearts
Perhaps dreams do come true
Creator, it's all up to you
It's all in your willing,
Not the humans that are
On a spree of killing

Oneness with Nature
Is our ancient way of living
We stand true to our Original Nation
Not the Canadian or American patriotism
Old military saying
Make the red man white,
And they be blue,
For every yin
There is a yang
In our prophetic views
Blue is cleansing
Red is purification
And great white is light
Together they bring the colour
Of peace, hope and balance

This is the beauty of purple rain,
It's in the spirit and bit of magic
The colour of wampums and sacred stones
It's in the love, pain and joys
Creators weep, cry and heal
Feel the warmth of magic tears
Fall upon all good life on earth
To wellness, healing and good health
In our hearts we sing the song
To all of Creation
All of our relations
Peace, hope and universal balance
Where there is a hope, there is a chance
Give forgiveness another dance.

Poem For Rita
(Inspired by Rita Joe's poem "I Wrote, Now You Write")

"It's been done, now you do"
This is how I say I love you
Nin mawi'salkik lnu'k
kisi wikika'pk nin nkamu'lamun[1]
Writing was my freedom song
Write the right, correct the wrongs
War of words, I fought with gentleness
Positiveness
Tiptoed not to offend
But now I say help
If it's incorrect
Step on their toes
With free will and testament
Your senses right
Right the wrongs
L'nu is beautiful
Our talk, our medicine
Let it flow
Until we reach oneness
With our earth
Our hearts beat as one
In sync
One for all
And all for one
L'nu
Heal
Live
Forgive
Adapt
Evolve

1 I love true people / I wrote from the light of my heart

KA'LOLIN[1]

Aged fine with time
Her ways, her own
Eldest of We'koqmaq
Ka'lolin,
Our Queen
Our Wabanaki Princess
Her smile so warm
Her talk like song
L'nu we see[2]
Speak your Mother Tongue
She would say
As we weave away
Sip our tea and nibble on
Fresh biscuits spread
With homemade jelly
She teaches
She's patient
Sometimes
She shares history
Other times
Kind lessons
She reminds
Every basket
Unique and distinct
Original
Never the same
We share stories
We smile
Brown wrinkled hands
So strong

1 Caroline
2 to speak in the Mother Tongue

We pull Lipkite'knapi[3]
With unique tools
Lapaso'kwon[4]
Makes teeny strips
Seems simple and easy
Until I try
Then I understand
The complexity
She's a master
Artisan
Linguist
Life experienced
Imagine
The knowledge
Of her L'nu'ness
Still unknown to me
I'm the child
Observing as she
Engineers the baskets
Weaves, designs
We braid sweet grass
Exchange new words
Many pass by too old
For our understanding
Sometimes
We ask, we repeat
We try but we keep
Forgetting many
Or twisting tongues
Some stick, many don't

Je Pe'skalamit[5]

3 strips of wood pounded from the log, which are then bent to make baskets
4 a tool with several blades used to cut the basket strips into several smaller strips
5 to sigh or take a deep breath

She worries
She worries deeply
About the tongue
We make jikijijk[6]
They are pretty
And rewarding
The snail-like curlies
On the baskets
Sip more tea and biscuits
Inhale Auntie's switte'l
What we call
Sweet grass
A scent always
Warmly welcomed
Comes with spirit
And always
Magnificent
Diverse
Embrace the old
Traditional ways
Speak our Mother Tongue
Honour our elders
Be natural
Nature Na Nesta'wek[7]
Good spirit is nature
Our Elder says
It feels good
She praises our baskets
We honour her
The keeper of
Original L'nu ways
Keep them well
For we need them

6 snail; also, the curls on the baskets because they are shaped like snails
7 good head on their shoulders, naturally good

For our children
And their own
Her messages
Delivered
Between the lines
And Spirit
Receive and embrace
Weave away

Msit No'kmaq[8]

---

[8] To all our relations, all of Creation

Clayton Paul

Clayton Paul was born in Truro and raised in Indian Brook when it was still called Micmac. Before that, it was simply called Indian Reservation #13. Whatever name it went by, L'nu Sipuk has always been home. Clayton grew up in a variety of places, including Maine, Massachusetts, and Montana. He found Boston a city of ideas, some of which changed his life and made him who he is today, and in Montana he finished high school and picked up a trade while doing so. The person who influenced him the most was his mother. She taught him to read by hiding comic books in her apron pockets until he begged her to let him read them, and she was the bravest person he ever met.

Clayton's life has not been easy. His mother died when he was fifteen and a few years later his brother was killed in Boston. His father died of lung cancer. His two sons died within a year of each other. It has taken a while to get comfortable with the idea of being a survivor. However, Clayton recalls that when his oldest son needed him to appear in court, he did so, despite knowing he was wanted by the courts himself. The thought that he stood up for his boy when his son needed him makes him stand straighter today. Clayton has been clean and sober for twenty-five years. His family, extended family, and friends have gotten by on laughter. Together, he says, they've whistled while they walked by the graveyard, laughing until the stinging went away.

Gas Baggin'

One grey morning, a small group of my friends and I were standing around in the band office parking lot gas baggin' about money. We grew up poor on the reserve, so it's not surprising that when we have more time on our hands than the jingle of a few bucks in our pockets, the conversation eventually gets around to cold hard cash. In fact, since most of our knees have gone bad through work or sports, talkin' about money – who's got some, who's gettin' some, and tryin' to figure out how can we get them to give us some – has long ago replaced road hockey as one of our favourite games.

It has been said that our brand of gas baggin' is abusive, but we know that road hockey is, too. Frustration and boredom make for a volatile mixture. On the reserve, it also can be said that for us, gas baggin' has become a necessary evil. Somewhere in the middle is the view that gas baggin' is the way we "rage against the dying of the light" old-school style.

The game really took off when we heard in high school that the ancient Mayans played ball with human heads. It was around that time we decided to take the same bloodthirsty approach when we played our game. We may tease each other mercilessly, but, like any other contact sport, there are a few basic rules we follow. One of the few things that will stop a game is if a player gets way too personal with another player. Provoking someone to the point where they'll take a swing at you takes all the fun out of playing it. That's really about all that will do it, though. Even if a player takes a shot to the head, bursting into tears will always get him disqualified and suspended from future games.

Being spiteful doesn't do any of the crew any good. We all know life on the reserve can be hard and we see the inequity around us all the time. It's the little victories that count. To play the game well, a person has to believe that money isn't everything. The great players know that no amount of money can buy the truly important things in life. Winning the game doesn't always follow the same straight-line path. In an ideal setting, at the end of a scrimmage, a sort of moral conclusion should be reached.

When we take the high road, our game reminds me of an irreverent talking circle, or a group of old truth-speakers we had in some of the old cultures. But when we get carried away poking fun at the power and control that money buys on the rez, the gas baggin' can be a lot of fun. Playing helps us to blow off steam and generally helps to keep our feet firmly planted on the ground. If only by fuelling our imaginations, gas baggin' about the powers that be has become our homegrown brand of group therapy.

Despite our lofty ambitions to win a round, we're far from being a group of self-righteous moralists. Although we've tried hard not to become cold-hearted through the influence of money, we're hardly idealistic about the almighty dollar either. While we still believe that money is the root of all evil, we all know in our hearts that there's nothing wrong with having a few huge piles of tens and twenties lying around the house. It's not going to happen, though. We've long ago resigned ourselves to the fact that no one is going to drop a bag of money in our laps any time soon.

As long as the weather isn't too bad, we've found that the best place to gather highly combustible material to fuel our discontent has been, and will always be, the band office parking lot. As long as our people have been on this reserve, our overall economic well-being has been conjoined with the band office. For better or worse, we feel we've got a lot invested in the people who work in that building. Sometimes, we expect too much from them and maybe not enough from ourselves.

For example, we've chewed the flavour out of the topic of brand new cars and trucks parked in band councillors' yards years ago. We tend to forget that we had a say in who runs things inside the band office. Call it envy, but over the years, new cars bought in an election year have always made good kindling for sparking some incendiary conversations about who's making how much cash. When the local car dealer approved a boatload of car loans on the reserve, it threw off our game for a few days. That is, until we found another event to sink our teeth into and there's usually something going on to spark our interest. We've spent a lot of mornings standing around in small clusters in the band office parking lot listening to all kinds of second-hand stories about the legislated sums of money floating around the reserve. From the recent questionable fishery agreements signed to the equally questionable residential school settlements being paid, if what we can see bothers us, it's what we think we're seeing that seems to bother us even more.

Because of the broader range and the greater number of Native people those issues impact, we talk about those two issues more often. We all have friends and relatives who have been arrested as a result of being on the water and also as a result of being in the residential school. But we're a reasonable group of friends, too. We're working men and some of the guys have been in "the resi." We often talk among ourselves and from what we've seen in the newspapers, the jury is still out on certain fishery agreements. We're partial to the residential school survivors' predicament, and we've agreed that the residential school survivors have been to places and seen things we'll never have to experience. The general consensus is that someone should have brought a bigger bag of money to the negotiation table.

What tends to make those kinds of situations all the more frustrating is that what happens to resolve those issues is out of our hands. We've never fooled ourselves about what is out of our control anyway. Those issues were never in our hands to begin with. However, we feel the unfairness of it all gives us the right to have strong opinions on the two subjects. As frustrating as it sometimes can be, complaining is all we feel we're able to do about certain issues. When pissing in the wind isn't enough, we return to "the game."

The morning's round began easily enough. One of the guys said, "There's never going to be a compensation package awarded for being born poor." Someone else shot back that he never expected any money for "being raised rez."

Being raised rez, he reminded the crew, means that, as a group, we've seen it all, and it's more than likely we can expect more to come. He pointed out that most of us could take almost anything that's thrown our way. By way of example, he used growing old and poverty as prime examples of the conditions of life on the rez. "Now, don't growing old in poverty just suck?" He looked at one of the younger men in the circle when he said it. It was the same as telling the young man who may have thought he was a tough guy that he wasn't tough at all.

Being new to the group, the younger man took the bait. Telling someone they were raised in harder times than these has always been a crowd favourite. We've always been proud that our grandparents lived through the Great Depression – the Dirty Thirties – by depending on their wits, rabbits and lusknkn.[1]

Common sense should warn a person not to poke the avalanche god in the eye with a pointy stick and folklore says that a person should never get into a conversation with a representative of mischief. Apparently, the young man never heard these nuggets of wisdom because he decided that rather than wear his silence like a badge of shame, he was ready to play the game with us.

---

1 lusknkn or lusky: homemade bread. Lusknkn comes from the word "ntlusknkn," meaning "my elbow," which the people used to knead and work the dough to prepare it for the oven.

Seeing he didn't know how to begin, someone asked him, "Well, how poor were you growing up?" The ball, so to speak, was in his court. To meet the challenge head-on, he would now have to come up with a suitable answer.

"Remember those big fifty-pound lookin' bags of fluff[2] our parents used to bring home? I was so poor, I never tasted Cap's Crunch cereal until I was a teenager."

The answer was good, but it was delivered by a rookie in rookie style. I should mention here that in the overall point system, form does count for something. The man on his right shook his head and replied, "Yeah? We had fluffs, too, but we ate 'em with water 'cause we were too poor to buy milk."

It was an impressive retort and from there on, the game quickly gained momentum and the cutting contest took on a life of its own. From the other side of the circle, someone said, "Oh yeah? I was so poor, I used to take hot dog water to school. Mum used to say, 'Take it! It's from last night – it's still good.'"

Then came the mandatory head fake delivered by one of the two brothers sitting on the curb in the shade. He pursed his lips to point at his brother and asked him, "Remember when we had to take lusky to school, and you tried to trade it for a baker's bread sandwich? You kept trying to convince the kid by telling him, 'No, really. It's cake.'"

With that said, his brother quickly found an opening. "That wasn't half as bad as when you tried to trade your sandwich made from bread loaf heels for something else. I remember you tried to sweeten the deal by telling the kid, 'Really it's a half-moon cake.' He looked you back straight in the eye and told you, 'No, it's not.' You told him, 'Yeah it is. Look! It's got jam in the middle.'"

---

2 fluffs: made from wheat hearts that were "popped" using heat, moisture, and pressure. They came in large bags that resembled small pillows in size and texture and felt like the kapok in personal flotation devices. Although fluffs didn't contain much food value, they kept many families afloat.

Not to be outdone, he shot his index finger directly at his brother's nose and said, "You made the trading harder when you brought burnt lusky to school 'cause there wasn't enough flour to make another batch. That same kid looked at you with the stink eye and told you, 'My mother told me not to trade with you.'"

With the opening salvos out of the way, it was on to the lightning rounds where we threw out topics from the tops of our heads. Everyone who has lived in a temperate zone has used empty bread bags as waterproofing for socks, so it's never really counted for any kind of substantial point total.

But the other universal crowd favourites are the stories that come from having wogs as a kid. On the school bus, we even went so far as moving away from some of the cute girls we used to have boyhood crushes on if they scratched their heads for too long. I remember even if their ears got cold, we weren't allowed to lend certain people our stocking caps. Without saying it out loud, we knew that some of those same people never made it past the age of thirty. We also knew deep down that in some of the school pictures yet to be taken, there will be some others who won't make it past thirty, either. I think poverty has a slow way of killing the spirit. It was a sobering moment.

Caught up in the good ol' days, the comments that followed began to take a strange reversal of direction. We talked about the bonding we experienced growing up on the reserve. As bad as taking lusky sandwiches to the white school was, and as bad as having to watch out for who was scratching their heads when they sat next to you in the old Indian day school was too, having had brothers and sisters in the same boat as you made it a lot easier to get through those bad ol' days. It was one of the brothers who brought it to the group's attention that it isn't a world made for going it alone.

For years, we ragged on the Indian politicians on our rez because where jobs are so scarce, the philosophy never followed was "cut from the top, never from the bottom." Short-term employment made it hard to plan for the future and shiny new cars in the yards of persons of position became a solid symbol of the division between the haves and the have-nots. It never helped matters when it all seemed like they were getting easy money.

As for the settlements for the residential school people, there was no argument earlier and there wasn't one now. The money they were paid came the old-fashioned way – through blood, sweat and tears. Now, that's another sobering thought.

While we were on the subject of the residential school, someone said they didn't have to worry about wogs in the residential school. We heard from a guy who was there that when a boy got bugs in his hair at the resi, everybody got a buzz cut. We all agreed that was cold and impersonal.

We all agreed, too, that being separated from their families for such a long time as the survivors were wasn't such a good thing, either. Maybe it doesn't make much difference to some people who's doing the beating-on or where it's being done, but it does to our small circle of friends. Personally, I'd take Kiju[3] and her hairbrush chasing me around the house over being cornered in a room by Mother Superior and her metal ruler any day. Looking at the situation in that light, the three square meals a day and the warm bed that were offered at the resi school doesn't look like a good deal at all. It made more sense when someone said three brothers under an old army blanket made for a warm bed, too.

After some serious blessings counted, we tallied up our point total for that morning's game. Most things considered, these are the numbers we came up with:

Signing a deal with the DFO: $25,000,000

Loss of language and identity from the diminishment of culture: $28,000

Being at home with your head in Mumma's lap while she cleaned the nits from your head: priceless

---

3 Mother

SHALAN JOUDRY

Shalan joudry is from the traditional district of Kespukwitk (southern Nova Scotia) and is of Mi'kmaw ancestry. As a child, poetry and a fascination with nature were her first loves that later led to storytelling, songwriting, theatre, and video production. She first published her poetry in a children's magazine when she was ten years old and has not stopped writing. Somehow, shalan freed herself of the confines of high school to undertake short quests in the woods of Kespukwitk and found her spiritual connection to nature on her own terms.

When she was ready, she ventured off to Ontario to complete a diploma in audio engineering, which led to work with a small video production company. Continuing on her journey, shalan studied performing arts through the Centre for Indigenous Theatre and the Banff Centre for the Arts (Aboriginal Dance). She worked on various projects with other Indigenous artists and has performed on small stages across the country with her piano, drum, spoken word, theatre and dance.

Because of her many interests, shalan must focus each phase of her life. Therefore, after she had spent some time in the arts, she returned to her passion for ecology. This led her to complete a Bachelor of Environmental Science at McGill University in 2005.

Since then she has been involved in community-based environmental and performing arts projects that she feels are founding components for healthy communities.

Shalan says, "I have travelled over all of Canada as well as abroad. I returned home to Bear River to become a mother and raise two imaginative daughters. I now learn from them, my beauties: Malaika and Milidow, wela'lioq. I give many thanks to many teachers and the history of the land. In this way, i, too, remember the words and life of Rita Joe."

The Challenge

it's all so fragile and i'm trying to believe
an indigenous worldview, custom, and knowledge
will survive the distance
between my grandmother and me

but it's late tonight and i won't make the sunrise
and tomorrow i will struggle to learn one more word
in Mi'kmaw
teach my tongue to soften at the back of my throat
and make scaffolding out of language
to hold up a nation once beaten into assent
and to go on

to believe we can remember
to believe that we will govern ourselves
be caretakers of Mi'kmaki once again
to believe i can teach my children
and that they will believe

Eastbound by Train

between the pages of sorrow i've kept waxberry
bundled with fir sap and ki'kwesuasqw[1]
i collected before leaving the East

i've been on the road for eight years
learning the lands, weaving relationships
gathering small gifts for medicine pouches
but the lessons of self-defiance
don't seem to fit in among the others

i tell a stranger these things on my eastbound train
and somehow my speech fades
from the opening doors i smell fresh rain
among the pines and remember Banff
when i danced
as alive as the Atlantic waves

he didn't believe my world
that we can turn against ourselves
holding mirrors in the place of truth
grow cocooned and come out the other side singing

did i share too much, you wonder
my poetry so private
my medicines too dry now to show others
without crumbling

but i knew he wasn't fully committed
and in a year or two he wouldn't remember my name
he'd only remember how he hates the train
all the way to Winnipeg

---

1 muskrat root

i remember the smell of pine sweeping in
and how soothing it was to fall asleep
with one hand in the middle
of writing this

Mourning Song

i arrived empty-handed
at the door of my brethren
having failed the foresight of service
offering then only the peaceful nature of ordinary things
like sadness

i imagined feeling pitied
standing there looking in
elephantly out of place
and yet i held my space
there among my sisters
i sat stiff and hip-joined
merging with their mourning songs
that precede death

i obey this kind of power
not because they are wise
but because they are holy

when it was my turn to lead
my voice faltered, forsaking me
so that there were only the drums
singing
for a whole round
we let the beats resound in the room
the vacancy of chant like a failing body
the song beating against the walls
of such a structured place
wanting free
like spirit
on its way out

(Untitled)

The most sacred treasures from Creation are void of name
They come shaped and we make use of them
    like medicines, landscapes, shared time

If we take this circle and smudge,
the vow of trust, give each other the precious gift
of time and space,
then together we allow each other to heal

Close your eyes, brothers, sing it out
and let that be medicine to walk away with
Close your eyes, sisters, listen to each other's stories
and let that be medicine to walk away with

Pass the stick and smudge again, together we will pray
Up in that smoke is our sorrow and sense of defeat,
leaving us lighter, higher, awakened,
so that we return to our labour,
let no one keep us down,
for this work is that which will carry our grandchildren
onward

Msit No'kmaq.

Where Wild Things Blow

I want my children to smell of forest
permanent balsam on their heels
spruce boughs scattered on their floors instead of carpet
their windows plagued with cracks
where wild things blow

How do i teach my children that everything is poison?
the paint on their blocks,
their plastic tea set
How do i prove the only remedy is hidden deep in the forest
that we must live here in the woods, find springs
befriend salamanders, pick berries
to be well?

As a mother, i see this land anew:
with every injustice, my womb aches
when salmon fail to return to the branches of our river
my womb aches
and i want to be that river, swell up with habitat
quicken the current again, blow oxygen, filter out the sand
give birth to time

I am a mother, like the land is Mother
and our children are each other's children
my daughters belong to the river like kin
and journey home through the thickest of forest
where wild things ebb and flow

Previously published online in January 2009 on http://brownroad.squarespace.com/brown-road-poetry

BROTHER, MAY I WALK WITH YOU A WHILE

Brown-skinned brother labouring down the hill
with your ash pack basket strapped on
your lean-lined frame, eyes dark moons drawn down
sustained to the ground
your old coat is poison-stained
a shadow so long behind you
stretching thin like elastic, coupling you here
unyielding
no matter how far you progress

Brother, may i walk with you a while?

A pole for trekking, scavenged by your bare hands
Swing, swing, like a metronome
to guard with conviction, a shield
from anything too temperate, too generous
So she'll leave some baked goods at the doorway
Take them with you, sweetheart,
Don't go hungry
But i know he'd rather be hungry
It moves you forward, keeps the pace

Brother, may i walk with you a while?

Now i've heard the stories, given you space,
kept to the right side of roads
But when you left your mind, brother,
you damaged mine
One late night, and chance
But now i've heard the stories, given you time
kept the right side of peace
But i have yet to hear your voice
May we walk together a while?

A Ceremony for You

I've watched the Grandmothers wait
and i want to be their pupil
tell them i've arrived
bring us into gear and start rolling
But i've been too many things for too many people
i'm a tourist here too

Let me give back something, in the waiting
I would give anything
    my song, my blood, my hair
to watch the process become whole again
Like a missing puzzle piece under the sofa, the people
would be circled about you listening
There must be a ceremony for that
the fragile anticipation persisting

I've watched them run out of time
or run out of sand in the hourglass
but then later they've somehow flipped themselves
to continue flowing
There must be a ceremony for that
the renewal

I've watched them teach
and teach
and wait
and teach
sometimes the change doesn't come
or the pupils stop coming
    they're *busy*, they say
And i want to weep for the world, our whole history
for our collective loss
But i have not been here long enough to know that endless trickle

of sand, how to cup it, how to flip
over

I have been here long enough to know
there is a ceremony for that, giving back strength
to honour our teachers

Patricia Doyle-Bedwell

Patti Doyle-Bedwell, a Mi'kmaq originally from Bangor, Maine, has directed the Transition Year Program at Dalhousie University in Halifax, Nova Scotia, since 1998. She is a lawyer, an author, and most importantly, the mother of Mike and partner to George. Patti has taught at Dalhousie University Law School and the School for Resource and Environmental Studies. She is a former chair of the Nova Scotia Advisory Council on the Status of Women and the past director of the Program for Indigenous Blacks and Mi'kmaq at Dalhousie Law School.

Patti's passions include justice for Aboriginal peoples, education and women's rights. She has served on the Canadian NGO (non-government organization) team to the United Nations on international women's rights and the Steering Committee for the National Association of Women and the Law. She earned a B.A. with Honours in Sociology and Social Anthropology at Dalhousie as well as an LL.B and LL.M. Her master's of law degree thesis focused upon compensation for residential school survivors. Patti also participated in the Governor General's Canadian Study Tour in 2000 that included travelling through the Northwest Territories. As well, she taught classes on Aboriginal peoples and human rights in the Faculty of Law at Sweden's Lund University. The late Canadian broadcaster Peter Gzowski selected her as one of "The Best Minds of Our Times."

Patti is a certified instructor in the Bujinkan Martial Art and has earned a fourth-degree black belt. She co-owns the Doyle-Bedwell Bujinkan dojo in Dartmouth with her husband.

And So I Turn to Rita

This is a story about resilience, strength, hope and courage. I am sitting at the dining room table in my apartment and I drift back to the times when I felt hollow and depressed. I read Rita Joe's autobiography, *Song of Rita Joe: Autobiography of a Mi'kmaq Poet* during a time that I felt no hope, no connection, weak and vulnerable. I found strength in her words. I began to feel the beginning of a connection that now sustains me, which I felt I had lost. Being Mi'kmaq demands we face so many issues; sometimes our own people attack us in the worst way. Who is Mi'kmaq? Who has the right to belong to the nation? Rita inspired me to find my place through writing about my perspectives and experiences. I have longed to be a writer, and in this story, I explore the impacts of my experiences and my upbringing upon my journey as a writer. Identity, truth, law, and my upbringing have all shaped my perspectives and experiences. Through Rita's writings, I learned to walk gently. She taught me what it means to be a Mi'kmaq woman and a writer.

I am Mi'kmaq. Some people believe that I am not Mi'kmaq enough. Others have placed me in an academic box without realizing that my Mi'kmaq roots remain strong regardless of my schooling. What does it mean to be a grassroots person? Does my experience of poverty, violence, sexism and racism disappear when I earn my degree? No, it does not, but living within such oppression taught me more about my values and culture than I ever thought possible.

I am fifty-two years old. Sometimes I still feel like a teenager. I have struggled with my past and my fit in the Mi'kmaq community. Both my mother and Rita Joe inspired me to find my place. My mother taught me to find strength within and encouraged me to stand strong and proud. Rita taught me to go inwards, to find my voice. So with shaking hands, I will tell you how my mom and Rita fundamentally influenced my life.

I grew up in Maine but my mother, Harriet Doyle, was from Chapel Island, Nova Scotia, born on the reserve and part of a family of eight. When my mother was six, the Indian Agent removed her and her younger sisters, Mary and Theresa, from their home to attend residential school. Unable to speak English, she and her sisters arrived at the school with barely a clue as to why the Indian Agent sent them there. Attending the school for ten years, my mom lost her language and her connection to the community – but she did not lose her Mi'kmaq heart.

When she died at age eighty-seven in February 2011, she was a small woman. As a child, I did see her as larger than life. Widowed at an early age, she had strict rules and she enforced them. She wanted better for her children. She spoke to us in English but we learned Mi'kmaq words. I grew up off the reserve because Mom refused to have us educated in Canada. I didn't understand why. We lived in a white community but she made sure we knew our Mi'kmaq family. From her, I learned about the values of the Mi'kmaq community and our need for family relationships, community and healing. But for a very long time, my understanding of my culture remained muted, unspoken and the only normality I knew. I could not explain to anyone what I understood my Mi'kmaq upbringing meant, only that "we are different from white people."

When my sister, Helen (known as Angel), and I were children we always travelled to the reserve. One summer, as we were driving there, Mom said, "Let's stop at my old school." At this point, 1969, the government had closed down Shubenacadie Indian Residential School the year before, but the building still stood tall and intimidating, a testament to the pain and horror experienced within. Dark, spooky and musty, the Shubie School enveloped me with fear. The darkness seemed stronger than Nagooset (the sun). I had never seen a school so dismal.

I couldn't believe such a school existed. As a child, I thought, "Oh, how cool to go to a boarding school." My only experience of boarding school came from TV and books. I felt that my mom must be very special to attend such a school. Certainly, she was special but not for the reasons I thought about as a child. The school did not look like what I imagined it would be.

My mom had little formal education but she pushed us to get one. She rarely shared her experiences of residential school with us but taking us to Shubie when we were children made me realize that she did not attend a boarding school congruent with my young self's vision of what one should be like. The halls were dark and dirty, the dorms huge and unfriendly, while the kitchen and dining room looked more like a prison than a school. At age eleven, I began to wonder: What was it really like here?

Although I grew up off the reserve, we travelled to my mom's community at every opportunity. I had glimpses of the differences between good old Bangor, Maine, and Chapel Island. We seemed to have more family members, we opened our home to people from Nova Scotia who travelled to Boston, we heard Mi'kmaq spoken in our home and we maintained our family connections. There was definitely a difference in our family connections compared to most of my friends: more people, more cousins, more travel to see them, more people staying at our house. As well as hearing the Mi'kmaq language spoken at home, we also experienced the values of the Mi'kmaq community. Of course my sister and I accepted this as normal.

As a teenager, I never recognized Mom's strength. She was a single parent, disconnected legally from her community due to section 12(1)(b) of the Indian Act, which decreed that marriage to a non-Indian stripped a Native woman of her status. (However, Native men who married non-Indians retained theirs.) None of us had status under the Indian Act. However, our family ties remained intact. We learned some words in the Mi'kmaq language, but Mom insisted that we speak English as that would be more useful to us.

Now, I marvel at my mother's strength. My dad died when I was seven and I became very ill. Recently widowed, left with two kids and no money, she also had to deal with my illness while facing her own grief. We moved into a little apartment across the street from our school. There was no phone. I remember the struggles we faced as children and the perseverance my mother showed throughout the time she coped with the loss of her husband, our father, in a time when society did not support single parents.

My mom talked a bit with me about residential school when I was older. I asked her why she still believed in the Catholic Church, and she told me that Shubie could never take away her belief in God. This tells me that despite the horror of residential school, the genocide attempted there, the goal of assimilation, Mom kept her Mi'kmaq spirit and heart. She has passed that down to us.

My mom always stood up for us, against racism, against poverty, against abuse. I know that I broke her heart many times as I moved through my life. She always had words of wisdom for us. Get an education, don't depend on a man, and make sure you can take care of yourself. She had a sharp wit and a sarcastic tone. At eighty-seven, she still had all her faculties and could zing you in an instant. I have learned from the best. She had an inner strength that sustained her for over eight decades.

If I had to describe my mom in one word, it would be strength. No matter what life threw at her, she managed to survive and thrive. She convinced me to speak out, to stand up and never take anyone's bull. I remember when I was twelve years old and I had passed in a history test. Because I was last in line, the nun ripped up my test and told me I was nothing but a stupid Indian. I sat at my desk and cried. I went home that day and told my mom what had happened. She got in our old car, drove to the school and gave the teacher a piece of her mind. I felt protected. I recognized her strength in standing up to the teacher. She told me, in no uncertain terms, that I should never let the bastards get me down. This mantra repeated itself in my mind as I attended law school at Dalhousie University in the 1990s, when I experienced racism at a level of insidious, powerful stabs. Never before had I met people so limited, so conservative, so narrow-minded.

If I could choose a second word to describe my mother, it would be courage. She faced not only many illnesses and losses but also death. A serious car accident ten years ago put her in the hospital. The doctors told us we might lose her. But she rallied and survived. My nephew died ten years ago. I was certain Josh's loss would kill her. But again, she rose up and survived.

If I could use another word, it would be faith. Her faith in God inspires me. Many times I have faced racism and discrimination. Her faith has sustained me when I didn't believe in the Creator. She was one of the Mi'kmaq women elders who washed and dressed the statue of St. Anne, the patron saint of the Mi'kmaq people, for the Chapel Island Mission during our annual gathering.

When I attended law school, I faced exclusion. I attributed their racism to my faults. If only I was smarter, better, shorter, perhaps I could gain their friendship. So, in an attempt to open myself up and be friendly, I began school by saying hi to my classmates, who ignored me. I felt like I was in high school again. It doesn't surprise me that the current climate of conservatism and the uncaring, hopeless attitude exists because I have seen people act in similar ways in law school. Law school professors told us we would be future leaders. But the degree from Dalhousie apparently means little if one is a racial minority. Or even an Indian.

Moreover, mainstream educators often judge multicultural processes of education as inferior. For example, graduates of Dalhousie Law School who entered their legal studies through the Indigenous Blacks and Mi'kmaq (IB&M) Program face discrimination from both the mainstream (somehow you got in the back door with no qualifications) and from the Aboriginal community (if you got through law school, you can't be Indian anymore). Dalhousie Law School aims to assimilate and acculturate students into the profession of law, while ignoring the cultural foundations of minority and Aboriginal students. I studied law to find justice but instead I found oppression.

As Patricia Monture-Angus states in *Thunder in my Soul: A Mohawk Woman Speaks*:

> When I enrolled in law school, I honestly believed that Canadian law would assist Aboriginal people in securing just and fair treatment. This is why I agreed to study law. Since then, I have learned that the Aboriginal experience of Canadian law can never be about justness and fairness for Aboriginal people. Every oppression that Aboriginal people have survived has been delivered up to us through Canadian law. This is true of the taking of our land and our children. Residential schools were established through law. The same is true for the outlawing of our sacred ceremonies and what is currently done to our people in the criminal courts of this land. What I learned long after my law school graduation was that Canadian law is about the oppression of Aboriginal people. My years in law school were so painful because oppression, even if only in study, is a painful experience. (p. 59)

Law school strips students of their personal perspectives. Somehow, I had to write papers and exams without showing who I am. The law school reduced me to a number. Do not write anything that will identify you. I found that quite difficult and oppressive. Yet law school, while painful, also taught me a fundamental truth: I am a Mi'kmaq woman no matter what anyone says. I also discovered that I could write from my perspective, through research and essay courses. I also found inspiration when I attended the launch of *Kelusultiek: Original Women's Voices of Atlantic Canada*, a book of Mi'kmaq women's writings. I cried when I heard the truth and feelings of the Mi'kmaq women who wrote with their soul. I cried because they also spoke my truth. I discovered the powerful nature of telling our stories, writing our truths, and standing up for our realities.

I have always wanted to write stories of my experiences, and I have struggled to connect my academic work with a strong grounding in my own life. Yet I hesitate to call myself a writer. To attach that label to the many labels that society has affixed to me, both positive and negative, feels a bit dishonest. I resonate with Rita's description of setting pen to paper while raising her children, where the label of "writer" and "poet" did not fit comfortably with that of mother, Mi'kmaq woman, grandmother. But she continued her writing, amazed at the honours she won because of her simple, powerful poems. She only described her life, what it means to be Mi'kmaq, how white society continues to oppress us, but she never gave in very long to the discouragement she faced both inside and outside her community. She believed she could educate the mainstream. She believed her poems could be the link between the worlds. If only the mainstream understood us, racism may disappear.

I met Rita Joe in 1979 when I was twenty-one. I told her my name, that I was Mi'kmaq from Chapel Island, that my mother was Harriet Doyle. I asked her how I could become a writer. She simply smiled up at me and said, "Write." The answer could not be that simple! I said thank you. Who would be interested in what I had to say? I still had unspoken dreams that I felt too scared to pursue. Writing must be more complicated than that. Writing meant I had something to say. I didn't think that I could speak from my experiences. Who would care?

So I kept journals. I have journals since fifth grade. The blank page offered refuge. At times, the blank page seemed like a deep black hole. It takes courage to face the void. The silence of that blank page does not allow me to be someone else. Whatever comes from my pen must reflect me, whether I am writing an article, a poem or an academic paper. Of course, law school ruined the blank page as refuge. My writing no longer created a safe space for me. I lost the power of writing my truth in law school because law school tried to strip me of my words. When I started my LL.M, I tried to regain my inner writer.

I chose as my topic educational policy and residential schools. Healing for me has meant regaining my voice through the written word – to purge the pain of doing my LL.M. thesis and having my committee see it as simply a "Patti had to get this off her chest" project. In fact, my thesis felt like a medicine song to me, my search for purpose and meaning guided by my ancestors and the Creator. During the research, I found the letter my grandfather asked the Indian Agent to write, requesting that his daughters come home for the summer. My mother had not known about the letter. With this discovery, I was able to convince Mom that her parents had not abandoned her as she had believed. My thesis work was my family/tribal story and the legal story woven together as one. I felt that I was on the path my ancestors provided for me as a writer and a lawyer. And to have those in power dismiss my thesis out of hand devastated me.

Exploring what it means to be a writer means facing the negatives. Discriminatory stereotypes haunt me. I never experienced subtle sneaky racism until I moved to Canada. I wonder what it will take to completely disengage myself from the opinions of the oppressive society that demands we maintain the status quo. No longer do we have to depend upon white people to put us down.

I have internalized the negativity that leads to depression and lack of motivation. I feel fear sitting here at the computer. I shake inside when non-Native people spout off about our lack of writing skills, or any academic skills at all. I want to remove writing from the list of the impossible accomplishments and instead create a safe space for Mi'kmaq people to write their stories, keep their journals, to publish their truth.

Ah, the truth. What is our truth? Each person must begin from his or her own personal experience. Rita did just that. Her poetry explored and defined what it means to live as a Mi'kmaq woman in a world that ignores our truth. As long as writers share ancient cultural knowledge, focus upon the past, maintain the Indian from the past, the status quo remains intact. Speaking the truth about racism, oppression, and the ongoing impact of living with the social problems that flow from poverty and discrimination has the potential to further marginalize the Aboriginal writer. Yet Rita exposed her truth and her reality of living as a Mi'kmaq woman in the twentieth century in a gentle, non-threatening way that allowed readers to share in her world, without feeling attacked. Rita showed us how to speak powerfully, share our stories, in a way that left the reader whole. Rita epitomizes to me the phrase "Speak truth to power." She did not hide her pain and joy but instead elevated her experience to literary masterpieces.

When I write, I am always concerned with the impact of my words on others. I wrote an article, "Justice as Healing," in *CAUT* (Canadian Association of University Teachers, Issue 44, April 1997) about my negative experience at the law school in 1997 when I was in so much pain from the loss of my babies. I also had struggled to be a good teacher at the law school in the midst of my difficulties. I hoped to make all of my students happy. I wanted to be the best, but I feared that I wasn't good enough, that I was in over my head. Yet I didn't face the fear, and despite my efforts, a student launched an appeal of my teaching. Losing a child devastated me, more so in the midst of teaching within an environment that rebelled against me.

When Professor Bankier asked me to submit my article about my negative experience at law school for publishing, I was home recovering from yet another miscarriage. I had to take some time off when I lost my second baby. I needed to find my spiritual strength again. I had to take the time to nurture myself, spend time with my family, to allow my body to heal completely. Wise people advised me not to publish that article, saying it would be better to wait until the pain had dissipated. I thought that publishing my article would exorcise that pain and the isolation I felt at the law school, isolation borne out of the grief I was experiencing at the loss of my children, and the struggle to maintain my voice, myself, and my credibility as a teacher. However, publishing the piece at this time was a mistake. I did not believe the good things told to me but I certainly very quickly believed the bad.

When the article first hit the press in 1997, I experienced much backlash at the law school. People felt that I was painting Dalhousie as a racist place. People also felt that I dismissed the support I received at the law school, during the appeal process and the subsequent rejection of the student's appeal of my teaching. I never meant to minimize the support I received from my teaching colleagues. The pain over the appeal coupled with the pain of losing my children and the struggle to be a good teacher contributed to the absolute fear that I had failed yet again in pursuing my dream.

In my state of grief and loss, I was extremely vulnerable to the backlash. But my pain remained unacknowledged. Instead, I found myself trying to listen to the members of the dominant society express their outrage over my nerve to speak to the racism and sexism. I heard comments from people, even from people who present themselves as "equity champions," who felt insulted that I would dare speak of the pain of racism. I felt shame so deep that I did not know if I would survive. Fearing to face the hostility every day, I was afraid to write my thesis, hesitant to expose myself again to the negativity of the law school community. I realized I had silenced myself. I wondered if I had the strength of my convictions: to write from my experience, to use the law as a tool for justice instead of oppression, to find resolution in the words I wrote. Again, Rita and my mom gave me the power to continue writing, delving into that deep space within me.

In that deep space, I had dreamed of being a lawyer. I dreamed of being a teacher. I wanted to do both. During my time off in 1997, I found Rita Joe's autobiography. I read her story feeling her strength flowing from her words. I recognized that I carried the same values and I came from the same line of Mi'kmaq women. I recognized finally that the dominant society has always focused their destructive laws and policies upon Aboriginal women and children. I began to understand that my ancestors' fight to maintain the Mi'kmaq nation meant that we could be here today. I realized that Rita Joe found her inner courage to put pen to paper, to speak her truth and to empower women to find their own and to express it through writing, art, and living our Mi'kmaq values of kindness, sharing, caring, honesty and spirituality.

Elders have told me that my truth comes from within. When I started my Master's in Law, I pledged to research and to write from my experience; this promise shaped my work on my LL.M. thesis. The thesis certainly met the criteria of the law school as all three committee members approved it. But the experience of writing about residential schools excavated pain I did not know I carried with me. I wanted to see my family compensated for their suffering. I searched through the law, seeking a remedy for such overt racism, genocide and generational violence. Initially no one at the law school took my topic seriously. I doubt that my committee recognized the pain I experienced except to say that writing my thesis became a personal journey, not one necessary for legal scholarship. Yet my writing always flowed from my experience and my thesis reflected the interconnections of law, oppression and Mi'kmaq knowledge.

I have seen the light at the end of the tunnel. I have learned to trust myself. I have learned that my life does have value. I have learned not to let other people hurt me like that again. I have learned to lean on the strength of being a Mi'kmaq woman, that I can achieve what I dream of, despite the pain, despite those few people in my class who sought to hurt me. I received tremendous support from elders in the community who read my *CAUT* article in the *Mi'kmaq-Maliseet Nations News* and my thesis. They took the time to write me and tell me not to give up. I have not given up. I went back and faced the music. And in doing so, I learned that people listen, that people understand and I learned that giving up is not the answer. I have been very lucky; I have achieved my dream of becoming a lawyer and a teacher, with the support of my family, my community, my colleagues at the law school and the students. Only a few students disliked my teaching, but I allowed those few to hurt me.

Law school has been one of the most enjoyable, stressful, and painful times in my life. I had to find my inner strength through remembering the power of Rita Joe and my mom. I realized that law has been one of the tools of the government to keep us down. But I accomplished what I set out to accomplish: I received my degree, I taught the law the best way I knew how, and I survived my losses to return to the law school with my values intact. I wrote my thesis in the spirit of truth and pain, resilience and power. I refused to let the racism of the school lead me to failure.

Racism is an ugly word. It is so difficult to talk about it without people being hurt. That was not my intention. But racism does hurt, and until we begin to explore its impact on us, we will never begin to heal. We will never be able to detach from the dominant society's view of Indians. In traditional times, we had strong communities, and worked hard. We still need to work hard, to receive the education that at one time would have meant we would lose our identity as Indian people. Education in the mainstream gives us the tools to understand our own oppression, our history, and our values.

Part of my journey involves writing. Sometimes people will not like what I write but when I published "Justice as Healing," I needed to write about my pain. Whether it should have been published and used by others to hurt me further is another story. I will not make that mistake again. I will not purge my pain and inflict it upon others without taking the time to examine its impact on them. But at the same time, I will not allow others to silence me again or doubt my worth as a Mi'kmaq woman. I am trying to cleanse myself of the negative stereotypes that continue to haunt me. I believe that Mi'kmaq women must put pen to paper, to explore their lives and find their courage. If that is the path, follow it.

Education has always focused on white, mainstream, elite people. Racial minorities have faced difficulties in accessing justice. Case in point: the situation of Donald Marshall Junior, convicted for a murder he did not commit, and imprisoned for eleven years. His experience clearly illustrated the obstacles faced by Aboriginal people in the justice system. Dalhousie Law School, having trained many of the lawyers and judges involved in the wrongful imprisonment of Mr. Marshall, decided in 1989 to develop an admissions program, the Indigenous Blacks and Mi'kmaq (IB&M) Program for African-Canadian and Mi'kmaq students to increase the number of lawyers in both communities. In the Mi'kmaq community, no students had ever graduated from Dalhousie Law School.

One Mi'kmaq student likened the law school to residential school. The law school places extreme pressure on students to conform to the legal culture. Even when I started law school, the first essay I had to write concerned the dilemma of maintaining my voice and culture in such a hostile environment. As a professor of law, I learned first-hand that students from the mainstream culture expressed antagonism at my very presence. Certainly, as a student, I faced increasing hostility from those who believed I took a place away from a "qualified student."

When I started law school, I could not clearly explain what was different about me. I had attended a private Catholic high school, I had excellent grades, I did okay on the LSAT. I felt intelligent and I had a very successful Honours year in Sociology where I had the opportunity to do research that mattered to me. I felt confident and I also felt scared. I could fail law school. And this fear hung over me for the three years of my degree.

Through law school and my graduate work, while doing my LL.M thesis, I learned to hold on tight to my Mi'kmaq heart. I used the words of Rita and the experiences of my youth to disconnect myself from the racism at the law school. I discovered my value, my beliefs and I reconnected to the Creator.

I also recognized that I see the world holistically. I made connections between social policy, social justice and law. I soon learned that making these connections could be fatal to my academic success since many professors perceived critical thinking, especially in a holistic analysis, as fluff, not significant to the legal analysis. Mi'kmaq culture demands that I look at the world holistically and this way of thinking flows from our spiritual beliefs that everything is connected and has a spirit. Spirit has no place in law school.

Relationships with teachers, studies have shown, contribute to the success of Aboriginal students. However, most professors in law school remain very standoffish. The students (all) felt that I was very approachable and very easy to talk to, but the dean did not place any value on these qualities. Aboriginal students need to feel that their teachers respect them and will assist them on their learning journey. Teachers, as do elders, command respect in the Mi'kmaq community. Elders have lived wisdom they share with those who are younger. Teachers command the same respect and Aboriginal students will try to connect with teachers in the same personal way they would connect with elders. Often Aboriginal knowledge remains unspoken.

My LL.M thesis and the reaction to it silenced me for a time. I felt stuck and unable to move forward. So again, I went back to Rita. I read her book again. I searched for my voice. I knew that I had grieving work to do on my thesis. I spoke my truth but again felt the sting of disapproval. I felt excluded from the compensation discussions. I learned that some people have no honour, that despite the fact that the committee dismissed my work, many people benefited from the residential school experience suffered by my family. They dismissed my writing but then profited from it. I spoke to others about my thesis who congratulated me on not following a typical legal format. "You should be proud that you could intertwine your personal experience, Mi'kmaq oral history and legal analysis." Despite positive comments from other academics, I still felt ashamed of my work. The law school told me in no uncertain terms, "You are not good enough to teach here."

I ran to Rita's words. I began to find healing – that being Mi'kmaq and a writer is okay. That following my spiritual path means writing and speaking my truth. Rita Joe offered her words to all of us. While the dominant society gave her honours for her writing, I believe she ultimately wrote for her own healing and to find her truth. By sharing her experiences, she has given all Mi'kmaq women permission to explore their lives and truth. Her bravery has given me courage to reach out to the blank page again, if only to honour her with my words.

Rita also taught the mainstream society about Mi'kmaq culture. But I think her teachings lifted me out of the fear to write. The values of the Mi'kmaq community have persisted for a long time as well as our need for family, relationships, community and healing. Aboriginal women carry our traditions and our strength. I believe that our traditional knowledge and our spiritual power remain hidden and I had to search hard to find it within myself. The words of Rita Joe helped me to find the unspoken values I had grown up with. Even today, many of our spiritual leaders still denigrate women. The dominant society has twisted our spiritual traditions that recognized the power of Aboriginal women in our societies. Still, Rita spoke her truth about surviving, about being Mi'kmaq in the modern world, about the losses she experienced at residential school. She maintained her spiritual connection to our ancestors, which gave her the courage to speak her truth. She personified the strong Mi'kmaq woman, gentle yet courageous.

Often, I feel like I am nothing. I don't fit in either world. Sometimes, I cannot find the connection to my community because I don't speak Mi'kmaq. At the same time, I feel out of sorts with the dominant society because I feel trapped in a position that does not allow me time to pursue my writing and teaching. I find it hard to say that I am a writer. I find it hard to say that I am an academic. I find it hard to say that I am a teacher. I don't know if I have the courage to face the blank page when I feel I have little to contribute to the dialogue of Aboriginal women. Yet I believe in our power. I see clearly how the government tried to disconnect us from our communities through the Indian Act, through imported sexism and patriarchy.

But I am unsure of my role since I do not fit in either world. My own struggles mirror Rita's and at the same time, I hesitate to place myself there. Through her words, I learned to honour the strength of my spirit and the strength of the women in my family – those women who worked their fingers to the bone to provide for their children, who struggled with poverty and overt racism to rise above what the dominant culture thought about Mi'kmaq women.

In my experience as the director of the IB&M Program, I learned that mainstream professors still carry negative stereotypes about Aboriginal people. LSAT scores, GPA, community involvement, and successful pre-law completion did little to convince some professors that Aboriginal students had the qualifications to be there. However, I think cultural difference contributes to the difficulties Aboriginal students face in law school, more so than LSAT scores or GPA. The law school is a hostile environment. The professors look down on Aboriginal students, assuming they do not have what it takes to be successful. The cultural differences are seen as obstacles and little is done at the law school administration level to accommodate cultural issues. If one is accommodated, the stigma that accompanies it may hurt the student for the reminder of his or her time there. Professors' negative perspectives on Aboriginal students' skills and knowledge again places the blame on us, without those in power seeking to discover their own hand in the oppression of Aboriginal peoples. Mainstream society finds it much easier to blame the victim than look within.

Dalhousie reflects the nature of mainstream society, the good and the bad, like any other institution. I have somewhat healed from my pain. The wound has healed but sometimes the scar still hurts. I feel confident and alive again. I love working with the Mi'kmaq and Black students in the law school and at Dalhousie. I love teaching. I don't know if baring my soul though my writing will forever brand me as someone who is ungrateful, crazy or just plain unsuitable for the stress of academic politics. However, without the truth, our world remains stagnant, stuck in the past. Mainstream society may always see us through the lens of their negative stereotype. But the world is changing and we must persevere, as my mother did, as Rita did. It is up to every one of our Mi'kmaq sisters to reach out and encourage each other. I am still scared sometimes. So I sit and hope and pray that I have followed the right path. I pray that more Mi'kmaq women will follow our mothers' and Rita's example by living life with honour, kindness, honesty, and resilience. We need to tell our stories. Face the blank page and fill it with joy, love, pain, resolution and hope.

Laura Johnson

Mi'kmaq writer Laura Johnson is a member of Millbrook First Nation, daughter of Jane (Julian) and the late Stanley Johnson. She has been creating stories and poetry since the early 1990s. A recipient of the Maritime and Northeast Pipeline (M&NP) Scholarship and Academic Achievement Award in 2003, Laura is currently enrolled in Mi'kmaq Studies at Unama'ki College (Cape Breton University) in Nova Scotia, where she studies arts, history, and Aboriginal and treaty rights. She made the Dean's List in 2010.

Laura is inspired by spirituality, nature, and family, and her interests include music, science, and traditional artwork. She makes her publishing debut in this anthology.

One last breath

Waking up to chaos
And the smell of burning wood.
Hearts beating faster
Determining if it's a dream.
Every stride taken,
Is slower than the last.
Concernment and derailment
Occurs in the thoughts of loved ones.
The ones left behind are already dead.
It is a place where only nightmares come true.
Like a war veteran
Recovering dead bodies
But effacing more than one person
It affects the family's souls.
Spirits hovering around are
Helpless to the sound of
The gasping of one last breath.

Separate paths

What is said in silence
Cannot be put into words.
Bonds grow stronger but
Are forgotten in time.
I hope I'll never forget
This great friend of mine.
The one who was there
Through thick and thin
Reaching for our dreams
Down two separate paths.
This friendship will last,
For I'll hold you in my heart
When we start this journey
Down two separate paths.

Surreal

The beauty you have bestowed
Upon me has grown stronger
Over the years. In your eyes
The stars shine bright,
Giving me the strength of the moon.
You say things I only think of
And feel just like a dream.
The slightest touch from your
Hand touches me deep within my soul.
Could this all be true, this feeling
Of a surreal world?
Words are lost in the spur of
The moment of being with you.
You take me away from here,
But it is here that I have to stay,
Coming back for more and more,
Knowing the consequences of this,
Sharing a love that is ours,
Keeping our deepest secrets silent.
One day we'll run away, love,
Someday I can be with you.
Until then we'll just converse,
Communicate with our skin,
For when I look in your eyes
I feel like it'll just begin.
We'll fall for each other then,
So wait, my dear, for my love.
Don't leave everything behind,
Just remember what we have.
We'll fall in love in time,
Keeping our deepest secrets silent
Of communicating with our skin.

Apart from us

Today is the last day of
Having you around here.
Hugging our goodbyes forever
Feeling you deeper with this.
An angel gone astray
Is still an angel to me.
Blocking out the pain of
Not ever seeing you around.
No longer deeply communicating
No talk without words.
Simple sorrows let go of
Into the world like us.
The way we once were
Is now apart from us.

Souls Surfacing

The time it seems to slow down
But the years go by so fast.
Everything you can't remember
Is somewhere in the past.
When you feel death's fate,
Holding back the need to cry.
Sometimes we are enlightened
From the angels passing us by.
It's only a life experience
But our souls surfaced there.
Then I knew deep within me
That it was you who always cared.
Into the darkness of night
In my mind I prayed:
God, have mercy
And show me the way.
With feet on solid ground
My emotion gone astray
I looked at the world
And knew I was okay.
It was only a life experience
But my soul surfaced there.
Then I knew deep within me
That it was you who always cared.

ODE TO RITA JOE

Timeless words of yesterday
Are etched in stone
As you listened to the wind
For your stories and songs.
We shall do the same,
Honouring the ways you were
An original peaceful warrior.
The peace shall continue
In the eyes of our youth
And in the hearts of our elders
Reminding us of our home.

Theresa Meuse

Theresa Meuse was born and raised on the Bear River Mi'kmaq First Nation. As a single mother, she attended Dalhousie University and graduated in 1990 with a Bachelor's Degree in Sociology and Anthropology. Shortly after graduating, she went to work for the Confederacy of Mainland Mi'kmaq (CMM) and worked in areas of employment equity, social and health programs. She left CMM in 1997 and spent considerable time volunteering at her son's elementary school while working as a First Nation Educator and Advisor. She was a member of the Halifax Police Review Board for nine years. In 1998, Theresa received the YWCA Women of Achievement Award, which annually recognizes twelve women for their outstanding accomplishments. In 2004, she returned to the workforce with the CMM and next took a position as a health technician with the Atlantic Policy Congress of First Nation Chiefs (APC).

In 2007, Theresa was elected Chief of her home community of Bear River for a two-year term. In January 2010, she returned to her consultant work with a focus on cultural education. Theresa has undertaken a research project for the Department of Education, Mi'kmaq Service Division; developed cultural information for St. Francis Xavier University; assisted with a Mi'kmaq

Early Intervention Child Project; worked with the Halifax Regional Municipality Urban Aboriginal Strategy initiative; and completed a contract with Dalhousie University as the Acting Aboriginal Outreach Worker for the Aboriginal Health Sciences Initiative. Theresa is the author of a children's storybook, *The Sharing Circle*, and is working on several manuscripts for publication as well as providing services as a First Nation Educator and Advisor. Theresa is married, has three children and four grandchildren.

The Burial

An earlier version of Part One appeared in volume one of *The Mi'kmaq Anthology* as "The Chief." The continuation of the story is included here as Part Two.

Part One

In the 1950s, near an old gypsum mine in Annapolis County, the remains of three humans were uncovered. A museum archaeologist identified them as a woman of child-bearing age, a child about nine and an infant. The archaeologist found that the bones were two thousand years old and the incisor teeth were those of North American Indians. There is no proof the remains were Mi'kmaq, but as the Mi'kmaq were the first people of this area and the excavation site was near one of Nova Scotia's Mi'kmaq communities, the archaeologist assumed they were.

The Chief of the local community was contacted about how to deal with the remains. He spent a long time considering the best thing to do. After speaking with Elders and other friends, the Chief reached certain conclusions. As the remains were dated pre-Christianity, to place them in a formal burial ground, such as the cemetery on the reserve, may be considered disrespectful. Near the community was an actual traditional burial ground preserved and protected by a national park. This seemed like the best and most appropriate choice for burial of the remains. However, the Chief did not want any media publicity for the burial – he did not want to risk that curiosity-seekers would disturb the bones in their final resting place.

The Chief again sought direction for the type of ceremony to hold, for he wished to show the utmost respect for the remains when he placed them in the ground at the burial site. He received many suggestions but had to decide for himself what to do.

On the day the remains arrived at the reserve from the museum, he asked numerous people to go with him to the burial ground, but no one was available or willing to go. So he decided to go by himself. He placed the small boxes on the back of his truck and headed out to the site, wondering the whole time if he was doing the right thing. Upon arriving, he carried the remains to the gravesite and found the holes dug by the park keepers were too small. He immediately began to dig with his hands to make them larger. He laid the boxes in the graves and covered them with dirt, leaves and twigs. He did not want people to know that a burial had just taken place. The Chief hoped that the remains would now lie in peace. Unsure of exactly what to do next, he continued on to the best of his knowledge. He lit a braid of sweet grass and said what he thought were the appropriate prayers: he spoke from his heart. The Chief then left the gravesite, still not really sure if he had done the right thing.

As he walked the path back to his truck, he asked the Creator for a sign that he had done what was right and proper. Shortly after, the birds began to chirp loudly and the squirrels scurried and chattered. He thought maybe this was his sign, although he was hoping for something a bit more elaborate. He wasn't really sure if this sign meant to go back to the gravesite or continue to his truck. He paused and thought for a while. He decided there was nothing more he could do. He had to be satisfied that he had done the right thing.

As he got into his truck and closed the door, he looked on the side of the road and, to his disbelief, there stood a black bear – that was why the squirrels and birds were making so much noise. He began to think about his journey and realized that if he had chosen to return to the gravesite, he would have probably met the bear on the path leading back to his truck. The feeling he had at that moment told him that this was his sign. He was sure now he had done the right thing.

Part Two

In the fall of 2008, I asked the Chief to show me the land where the remains had been found so many years ago. He graciously took me to the site that stretched along the ocean's shoreline. We walked along the sides of the embankment, noticing the clam middens, still evidence of past lives. He explained the teachings of the clam middens and the teachings held such wonderful history of our ancestors. Middens can be an indicator of ancient dwellings or eating places.

When we arrived at the area where the remains had been excavated, the Chief located a flat stone and began digging in the earth. It did not take long before he had uncovered several stones and asked me to look closer. Not being sure what I was looking for, I picked up each stone and examined it. From the pile were two that caught my attention. One looked like it could have been used for chipping away pieces from other stones. It reminded me of a single bitted axe head. The second stone was long and narrow and one end was more bevelled than the other. It was tubular and reminded me of a hammer. Both types of tools were something commonly used by our ancestors, and I was excited to think these stones could possibly be their tools. I had an instant connection without clearly understanding why.

When I shared this experience with the Chief, he smiled and began to walk away. I quickly made an offering of tobacco to the site, picked up the two stones and started off to catch up to the Chief as he walked down the embankment to the shoreline. It had been such an honour and privilege to walk on the same soil as our ancestors. What a feeling of joy and yet a sense of sadness. What had happened years ago that caused those remains to have been left here? How many other ancestors are buried here at this site, now being used by the public for other activities? Despite the contradiction of my emotions, I felt such a connection to the lands and imagined my ancestors living along the shoreline. To this day, that very spot still makes me think back to that trip with the Chief.

When I arrived home, I placed the stones along the edge of my homemade fire pit, which was built to provide for a sacred fire. The stones represented the remains that had been previously found and then respectfully placed in a traditional burial ground by the Chief. My intentions were to host a four-day sacred fire someday, during which I would make sure the stones were acknowledged and blessed by the fire. Then I would maybe return them to the place where they were found.

Over the next several months, I would occasionally look at the stones lying at the fire pit and wonder if I should return them to the site. Doubt made me wonder if that was the proper thing to do or if I should have even taken them in the first place. I eventually decided to allow the spirits to give me my answer. Letting the spirits speak meant not stressing over what I was to do and when the answer came to me, I would know it.

The following summer I hosted a four-day sacred fire and many people attended. Throughout the four days I got to share the story of the stones. The teachings from some Elders were that the stones represented the Grandfathers and Grandmothers of our ancestors. This meant they held the wisdom of our ancestors and when heated, allowed for the wisdom to be shared with others. Everyone was intrigued with this cultural sharing.

People would go to the fire and some took the time to acknowledge the stones by placing sacred herbs. It was a beautiful four days of spiritual connection and even people from as far as Australia attended the closing ceremonies.

At the end of the closing sacred fire ceremony, an Elder spoke to me about the stones. She believed the stones should not be placed back at the original site; instead, I should keep them at the fire pit. I was grateful for her sharing her wisdom and agreed to keep the stones even though I didn't know why or for how long.

After everyone left the ceremony and I was alone, doubt began to creep into my thoughts once again. "Why is this happening?" I asked myself. "The Elder said to keep them, but for what purpose, for how long?" Just like before when uncertainty clouded my thoughts, I called upon the spirits to help me learn what to do with the stones.

That night I dreamed of three male community members who had passed away in the past couple of years. Two were prominent in the dream and one stayed in the background. When I awoke from the dream, I tried to make sense of it. I again wondered if the answer would come to me someday. Within a few days I had forgotten about the dream.

Three weeks later, our community had a guest speaker who shared his knowledge about rock and stone formation and its importance to our culture and history. During his presentation, I began to think of the two stones I had at the sacred fire pit. When he had finished his presentation, I asked if he would come to see the stones I had found. He graciously accepted my invitation.

After I shared the story of the stones, he picked up each one from its spot and examined them in detail. He explained that both stones appeared to have markings like artifacts found at other sites. The shapes followed the patterns of tools used during ancestral times. He told me that in ancestral times when someone passed on to the spirit world, their tools and other belongings would be buried with them. These stones could possibly be the tools of the remains that were previously buried by the Chief. He suggested that maybe the stones needed to be taken to the same traditional burial site to be with the remains. He also suggested that perhaps the spirits had called upon me to find these stones and take them to the remains. I stood in amazement and understood that this could be why my connection was so great from the moment I saw the stones at the site.

His words held so much meaning that in my heart I believed I had finally received my answer. I interpreted the answer as being that years ago Grandfather's spirit (the male chief) was chosen to bury the remains and now, Grandmother's spirit (the female chief) was chosen to bring the tools.

With great excitement, I asked the Chief if he would go with me to take the stones to the traditional burial site. He agreed.

A couple of weeks went by and I still hadn't made any plans for what day the stones would be taken to the burial site. Then I had another dream. This time it was about three females who had long passed away from our community and again two remained prominent. When I awoke, wonderment again crept into my mind. What did that dream mean? After leaving my home that morning I visited three women working at the local heritage and cultural centre. After I told them of my dream, it immediately came to me that both dreams were attempts to hurry me to get those stones to their resting place. At that moment I shared my thoughts with them and immediately set out to prepare taking the stones that very day to the burial site.

I phoned the Chief to see if he was able to go and with a little reluctance he agreed. After I hung up the phone, something was telling me not to take him but to take a female, maybe one who was a grandmother. I then phoned a fellow grandmother friend and she humbly accepted my invitation. When I shared this development with the Chief, he too thought that was the best thing to do. He described where to find the area where the remains were laid so I would know where to place the stones.

So I gathered all my ceremonial belongings and set out to pick up the other grandmother. She brought along her medicines and away we set out to the burial site. Upon arrival, we walked to the site and respectfully laid out all our belongings. Neither of us knew what we would do for a ceremony nor did we care, as we both believed the spirits would guide us.

We found the area where the stones would be laid and began digging a hole using smaller stones found near the spot. When we believed the hole was big enough, my friend played her drum and began singing ever so gently, while I prepared my medicines. We lit the sage and cleansed ourselves and the lands. We placed our offerings around the site and silently said our own prayers. I placed the stones in the hole and together we gently covered them. Just like the Chief did with the remains, we too wanted to leave the site in a respectful manner, making sure no one would know that a burial had just occurred.

We conducted a few other ceremonies, including some more drumming and singing. During our singing, the breeze gently made the leaves of the trees seem like they were singing along with us. It was such a beautiful moment and allowed us to know we had done the right thing.

I hugged my friend and thanked her for being part of this wonderful time. We both felt so grateful and honoured to have been chosen to bring the tools to their rightful owners. We were all now at peace.

We quietly packed up our belongings and walked back to the car. We couldn't stop smiling on the drive back home and knew we had just experienced something that was truly a traditional teaching, blessing and connection to our ancestors.

Female Chief

After graduating from university, I held a few positions for several years working for a couple of Mi'kmaq organizations, all of them governed by a board of directors, made up of Chiefs. As an employee I served as an advisor to and assisted with program development for their communities. This meant I had regular contact with Chiefs and communities at various levels. In these positions, I sometimes felt frustration as to why the Chiefs weren't showing more enthusiasm with the projects I was responsible for. I used to think that if I were a Chief, I would make these types of programs more of a priority and give them a lot more attention as a political leader.

Now, having been a Chief, I have come to learn that a Chief's life is busier than I ever imagined. For the first time I have a true sense of "24/7" as that is what the job entails. In order to stay on top of the many things that come to the Chief's table, I had to depend on the expertise of others to do the jobs that needed to be done. This dependency is vital to managing everything. I also had to place a great amount of trust in each person to do his or her job. These people are essential to the life of a Chief. Maybe that is how the Chiefs felt toward me – a person they could trust to get the job done.

Running for Chief was something I thought would never be part of my journey. I had family members who had been involved in the leadership for many years. Very seldom did their jobs seem fulfilling.

For a long time I lived off reserve but having the rest of my family living on reserve enabled me to visit the community often. Also, community contractual work helped me to learn more about band business. As a result, I felt that this allowed me to keep in tune with community living.

Then my employment experience added further understanding of how things worked outside the community and with government. My skills developed in areas of traditional understanding such as respect for Mother Earth, cultural spirituality growth and historical knowledge. As well, I learned office administration skills and program development and supervision throughout the years.

In 2007, the election was approaching for the community of Bear River First Nation and I was being encouraged to run for Chief. At that time, this was the only position I could apply for, as living off reserve prevented the opportunity to run for Band Councillor.

I didn't really take the thought of being Chief seriously at first and even joked about it to my family. Then one day, someone asked why I was not being so serious about this opportunity. After that, a few people whom I respected encouraged me to give it a try.

I spoke with family members to talk about what it would mean to our family life and its potential impacts. Everyone supported me except for my mother, whose opinion meant a great deal to me. She had concerns that this was a stressful job, and it would hurt her deeply to see me stressed out or being put down by someone because I was the Chief.

For several weeks I tried hard to convince her that everything would be okay. The turning point came when I shared that if the spirits wanted me to be Chief, then it would be. If not, then so be it. My journey would have something else for me to do. She continued to see my positive outlook and it wasn't long before she began to show me her support. We would talk about different scenarios a Chief faces and I would always assure her with a positive reply. We even got excited about me living with her in the community during the week if I were to become Chief.

It didn't take long for word to get out through Mi'kmaq country about me running for Chief. Many people shared their support and that inspired me to continue on with this journey.

The election was in November of 2007, so in October the nominations were announced, and there was my name in black and white. Seeing my name on the ballot sheet made me think, "Am I really doing this? Am I crazy?"

My belief in the spirits directing my journey allowed me to willingly accept the outcome – win or lose. I prepared a vision letter that explained what I saw as my role should I become Chief and shared that with as many people as I could. Things seemed to be moving along nicely.

Then, on October 31st, 2007, nearly one month before election day, my mother passed away. On that day, I had spoken to her on the phone at noon and at 3:30 that afternoon I got a call she was gone. Our family was devastated. Our mother was our foundation. How were we ever to stand alone?

For several weeks following the passing of our mother, the election was the last thing on my mind and I even considered withdrawing my name. Close friends and family continued to provide me with words of encouragement and slowly my spiritual strength began to return. Not too long after that, I was able to get back on my journey that allowed the spirits once again to direct my path. Knowing our mother was now in the spirit world helped to boost that belief and I found comfort in that thought.

On election day, shortly after the polls closed, a few friends and family gathered at a home in the community to await the results. We even joked how Mom was not going to be around to give me her vote and wouldn't it be funny if I lost by one vote. I remembered saying, "Oh well, Mom didn't really want me to run anyway and since she is now in the spirit world, she can control that more than ever." We all laughed.

Then the phone call came. We held our breaths while it was officially announced that I had won the election – by one vote. I remember immediately looking toward a family member and the thought of our mother came to my mind. I remember saying that I guess she voted for me after all. We shared a few tears and joy all at the same time.

In this election, two other female band members and I became the new band council that night. We made history in our community by being an all-female council. What made it even more appropriate is that we were all mothers, and two of us were grandmothers. In addition, I was the first off reserve candidate to become Chief in our community.

Together we made up the TLH Team. TLH are the first letters from each of our names and the initials stood for Tender Loving Hearts. Although administration was challenging at times, we always reminded ourselves of our dedication and the commitment we made as the TLH team.

My term was up in November 2009, and I chose not to re-offer in the next band election. Shortly after I again took up consultant projects, focusing on cultural education. The spirits have guided me to a great deal of fulfilling work, and I am grateful for the opportunity to have served my community, to have worked with many dedicated people, and to have been part of creating history. Being open to where the spirits guide you is one of the most valued lessons I have learned.

John Sylliboy

John Sylliboy is a squijinu on the path to becoming Ulnu in Wedabeksi Unimaki (Cape Breton District). John is from Eskasoni, the eighth of nine children of Mary and Simon Sylliboy. He is the father of five, three sons and two daughters.

O Canada

Innocent children learning old ways
abducted into forced labour camps
residential schools where
frosty warriors suffer
genocide genteelly applied
victims in the eyes of the world
heroes in mine
meagre compensation
no apology no healing
it is time to celebrate
their survival in song
and dance, give them
the honour they richly deserve

UL'NUKEEG

Our Forefathers tall and proud
well into many winters
yet able to lead the moose hunt
Animals will be harvested
their sacrifice for our people
will be acknowledged and honoured
the Animal's Spirit
not to be forgotten
as long as the Sacred Circle
of Life is shared between us

Ul'nu-agot-eek

The place of many Ulnu feet
was a place where people
lived long and happy lives
unhindered by want
serving only the needs of one another on the
journey to being Ulnu

This poem is dedicated to my granddaughter, Emily Maria.

David Marshall

David Marshall, born December 11, 1957, in Sydney, Nova Scotia, is the third oldest son of Caroline Marshall and the late Grand Chief Donald Marshall. David has lived all his life in Membertou. He is married to Terry Lynn Gallagher from Bangor, Maine. They share three boys together: Christien, twenty-five; James, twenty-two; and Julian, thirteen. David worked for the Membertou First Nation as a Native Employment Officer for the past twenty-six years and is now recently retired. He has also been a Band Councillor for the past twenty-three years. David loves his community and is dedicated to helping his neighbours. He frequently makes tea biscuits and lu'sknikn (traditional Mi'kmaq bread) for the elders, and, when he was working at the band office, for the staff. Since David quit smoking more than ten years ago, he has taken up Tae Kwon Do. He currently holds a third-degree black belt and is working towards his fourth degree.

David spends his spare time at his much beloved bungalow in Irish Vale, where he always finds something to do, whether it's fishing, swimming, walking on the shore, or enjoying a campfire at night. He welcomes family and friends to drop by whenever they are passing through, to share what he loves so much about Irish Vale.

The Passing of Kji Sagamaw

It was late August of 1991, and the forecast for that weekend looked promising. Before my wife and I and our children set out to go camping that Saturday, I dropped in on my parents. My father, Grand Chief Donald Marshall, had been diagnosed with cancer shortly after the New Year. When we arrived at my folks' place, other family members were present and the reception was somber, so I asked, "What's wrong?" My mom, Caroline, responded with a tremble in her voice, "It doesn't look good for Dad. Don't go anywhere this weekend."

I went upstairs and could not help but reminisce about my early days with my dad. I wanted to be so much like him. I always got so excited when he got home from work – just like the way my son waits for me. A father may not know it, but he is a hero to his child and that's how I felt about my dad. I will never forget when we would go for a drive in that panel truck or the Volkswagen buggy. I think we got a different car every six months or so. We weren't rich – it's just that back in those days, times were tough and we were lucky if the car my dad just bought would start the next morning. And if that wasn't the least of his troubles, he had a wife and twelve children to support. My parents were good providers, and I don't ever recall going to bed hungry. Wela'lin.

I saw my dad on the bed, which was very disheartening because he was once an outgoing, caring man not just to his family, but to all. Now he was bedridden and half the weight he once was. His decline took its toll on our family. He wanted us to continue on with our daily routines when his illness was first diagnosed, and he was very thankful for the kidney he received eight years ago.

I'll go back to the 1970s, which were a very difficult time for us, due to an incident in which a young man, Sandy Seale, was murdered, our oldest brother Donald Jr. was accused and within months was found guilty. On that very same day of the verdict, they wasted no time sentencing him to life.

Our family was pretty well left in turmoil until 1982. My mother would not submit, for she knew her son needed her, but she could not fully focus on the family. That's when we pitched in and grew up really fast. Our mom had a job to do, and we had no objections. My father, too, supported his son, and his wife's efforts. When Donald was exonerated a new life began for our family and the whole Mi'kmaq nation. My parents were in their glory and if it wasn't for my mother's perseverance, Donald would have probably served the whole life sentence. There were others also involved with Donald's release and we are very thankful to you all.

My father was Grand Chief for twenty-seven years. He was a man of great determination and he was always willing to help other families. He was looked up to. In 2010, a statue was erected in Membertou to commemorate him.

That Saturday, the Grand Chief struggled with every breath he took, and our whole family feared his time would soon be here. Some hysteria set in. Thanks to the palliative care worker and her guidance, order was restored.

His deteriorating condition was too much for us to handle, so we called for an ambulance to take him to the hospital. That was a difficult decision because he wanted to die at home. To this day, I still struggle with that. We stood by the Kji Sagamaw's bedside into the late hours and at about three in the morning my mother requested that she be left alone with her husband. We complied.

But for some unexplained reason, I had to go back. When I got there, my mom was singing in Mi'kmaq to our dad and as weak as the cancer made him, he still managed to reach out and give her a kiss and a hug. In all their years of marriage, I'm sure they had their moments, and that moment I had just witnessed was probably the most precious one of them all. It was a sad predicament for my parents knowing that the lifetime commitment to each other would very soon be coming to an end.

Amazingly, the Grand Chief made it through the night and was in good spirits later that morning. He had just gone through an ordeal we thought was the end, but when I entered the room there he was reading the newspaper, as if his brush with death just hours ago never happened. He pointed to a picture of the priest who had married him and my mother forty-two years ago – it was a nice reminder of that special day. After that, his condition took a turn for the worst, and although we did our best to make him comfortable, it was a losing battle.

My wife, our children and I stayed as long as we could. I told other family members to give us a call should any changes occur and we went home to rest. Just a few hours later my mom called and said, "Come down here. I don't think Dad is going to be with us much longer." Moments later my brother Terry called with the news that our dad had died. I put my head down and said, "No more suffering." We made our way down to the hospital to say our goodbyes.

Our sister Donna went on a pilgrimage with the Membertou senior citizens to Saint Anne de Beaupré, Quebec, to pray for the Grand Chief as his health declined. She went out of her way to tend to our father when he became ill. She did a lot for Dad, sacrificed a lot, and we are grateful to her. She was an inspiration to us during a difficult time. Wela'lin, and I mean that in every sense of the word.

It was hard to leave our father's bedside for the last time. We were all in a daze that Sunday when the Kji Sagamaw made his way to meet the Creator. My hero is gone. Rest in peace. He was a great man to his family and to the Mi'kmaq nation. Mi soqo Wulteskatulti'kapp! (We shall meet again!)

Mary Louise Martin

For the past sixteen years, Mary Louise Martin has lived a good life, a secluded life, on a small island in the southern Gulf Islands of British Columbia with her husband Gordon Hanson and her cat Solo. Her heart is split in two. In spirit, she has never left her family, friends and community of Millbrook Reserve and Atlantic Canada – her home, her people. The other half of her heart lives on the edge of the southern B.C. coast with her husband. The powers of the sea and the sky, the flora and fauna that surround her are a very important part of her life.

Mary Louise became a grandmother ten years ago when she and her son Sean were reunited after twenty-seven years of separation. Sean and his wife Laura Lee moved from Edmonton a few years ago and have made their home in Truro, Nova Scotia, with Mary Louise's grandson North (eleven) and granddaughter Lyrica (fifteen). "May their foundations be forever strong ..." Mary Louise's family of four sisters, three brothers, parents Ben and Jean Martin, and all her relations have welcomed Sean and his family as their own. The circle has been completed.

Mary Louise has a background in early education, museum studies, art education, and clerical training. She is a self-taught artist working with Mi'kmaq traditional materials to create her art. Her most recent artwork was purchased for the 2010 Winter Olympics (for both auction and venue site). Mary Louise has been employed in the arts and education on the federal, provincial, and band levels. Her poetry has been published in the first volume of *The Mi'kmaq Anthology* (1997), *Spirit of Wombman's Soul* (Nova Scotia College of Art and Design, 1984), and *Kelusultiek: Original Women's Voices of Atlantic Canada* (Institute for the Study of Women, Mount Saint Vincent University, 1984). "Grandmother Moon," a poem from *The Mi'kmaq Anthology,* has been adapted to music twice, the second time by Eleanor Daley from Toronto and published by Santa Barbara Music Publishing. A number of local poetry anthologies out of Pender Island, British Columbia, have also featured Mary Louise's poetry and prose.

PE'TE'WEI ... RITA

the fire is warm
there is a quiet in our home
the air is cool and grey outside
waiting for the kettle to boil
pe'te'wei ... rita
we will sit and write poetry together for a while

the whistle is singing
the kettle is ready
tea bags and water into the glass teapot
i bought at a second-hand shop
it holds a lot

tea begins to steep
instantly water turns
into amber then light brown reds
darker
darker
almost black brown
tea is ready
pe'te'wei ... rita
please
sit by the fire
and read to me
lusgi and wild blackberry jam
before we settle into a quiet afternoon of your powerful songs
wela'lin rita your gentle spirit is with me ...

all our relations in this world and of the next

RAYMOND (RAINMAN)

sweet fern from the east woodlands
he gathered some and brought me a bunch
once almost fifteen years ago
appears a clear visual in mind ever present
today

there was laughter
he is an elder
a friend
wise in his ways of the woodlands
and traditional knowledge
he liked to play tricks like coyote would
simply a child man of love
although he spoke his mind
and he was wise in times of troubled thoughts
visuals ever clear of yesterdays
here with me today

rainman
a deer man
held in time
captive in my mind

MI'KMAQ LIFE ON A LITTLE ISLAND IN SOUTHERN BRITISH COLUMBIA
from a little house through the windows facing eastward (a series of seven poems)

i
<u>the skyland above is very blue ... blue</u>
white clouds misted hang low ... fog
translucent but opaque covering the opposite bay
the south island across the bay ... disappear
low clouds ... fog travelling across the water
moving in closer pushing in against the large glass windows
(of this house on the edge of the rock cliff overlooking moody
    waters)
fog life takes form
all is misty and without notice
thick grey wall surrounds
if only for a while

ii
<u>storms</u>
rainwaters falling from skyland
winds tossing the cedar and firs
in a furious rush
then a hush
grey surround
storm today
not as wild as some

iii
<u>cold within</u>
cold day cold rainfall cold within lonely day
wind moves hard
fire dies with each flame whipping dancing inside the glass door of
    the woodstove
where will the next moment take this timeframe ...
hopefully away from this state of mind

iv
<u>dusk appears</u>
night meets day as day falls away
working together much like a water colour
darkness waits
undulating islands across the bay
outlines break the skyland and ocean
ocean mirror sky a solid grey blue
standing ones are black silhouettes against the backdrop of dusk
two lights glow inside the small house
cluttered and comfortable
wall-to-wall photos of family from far away
they are held captive in time
evening routine begins

v
<u>sleep and dreams come early</u>
morning comes earlier
coffee
day meets night
silently night is lifted away
lightly the wash of light grey is morning's water colour
the birds flutter for food from the trees and bushes to the feeders
the windows no longer mirror the interior of the house
it just happens gradually quickly
the routines begin
and with each day
all things great and small

vi
<u>new moon on the rise</u>
dauntless
dark moon arriving into night sky
navy sailors navigate their sage green vessels to poets cove across the bay
navigating by the stars perhaps not
overriding the creator's stellar formations is a guiding system they use via satellite
a man-made stellar creature that maps their every move through deep and shallow
mistress ocean of sojourns
usually one to three ocean vessels appear at poets cove across the bay
at times they arrive in fleets of seven or so
they announce themselves over a loudspeaker
in the grey precipitation or clear blue sunshine
during mid to late day
what do they do
cannot see completely

they stay overnight
sometimes they stay for two or three nights or so
but they always depart at 08:00 hours
in the grey of morning depending on the seasonal light
when they depart poets port
they maneuver their vessels heading towards the house (northwest)
turn eastward out of the narrow passage of the bay
most likely sail southwest returning to esquimalt naval base on vancouver island
they come and go from this little island winter spring summer and fall
ever since i can remember looking out the eastern windows now thirteen years ago

new moon on the rise
dauntless
dark moon arriving in night sky
(salutations ... grey wolf ... salute)

vii
<u>jip ji'je</u>
we live in a small house one large room windows with every exposure
large windows that reflect ... mirror windows of the forest surround
surround of the small house in the forest high in the standing ones
we feed the winged ones
sometimes
seeing the forest in the large picture windows
they fly into the mirrored image of the forest
and fall to the deck in stillness

some we are able to rescue
gently pick them up off the deck and wrap them with a soft facecloth
put them in a little cage and bring them in the house and keep them warm

we watch them and wait for them to come out of their sleep
and when they are really strong we set them free

others do not fall into shock
they simply perish of a broken wing or neck
we wrap them in soft tissue paper and bring them to a special
 place
where others have been buried before
make a small hollow in the soft earth mother
lay down some sweet cedar
and place jip ji'je down on the cedar bed facing east (gateway to
 the next world)
cover the winged one with more cedar and then place a rock over
 the tiny precious body
new life form
perhaps now they have completed their journey
perhaps they have passed through the mirrored glass
believing in their journey
it is not in vain
wela'lin niscum ... all our relations

FATHER SUN

father sun
light of skyland
golden hoop
you touch earth mother
warm and so loving

in the forest of standing ones
shadows dance through your light
stillness of the day
you enter through tree tops
and mingling boughs of evergreens
dapples of gold and yellow
dance onto the vernal earth mother

father sun
dear father sun
you are not far when skyland is a blanket of soft grey-blue
there is a light behind the veil of cloud ones
and rock people sing of silver and greys reflecting
we know you are there
dear father sun
we know you are there
dance with earth mother

father sun
keep us warm
you are the fire on a cold winter's morn
sweet harmonies with earth mother
most beautiful and powerful golden hoop
as it is you wish each day
i am your native daughter
wela'lin
dear father sun
wela'lin
ges'a'lu

MARIO

mario arrived on the corner of seymour and pender – vancouver, bc, sometime in late spring from quebec city in 2007. i wrote these narratives about mario in January 2008. i was told he was around then. in february 2008 i returned to vancouver to share these narratives with mario and he was no longer on the corner of seymour and pender. he has never returned. i have not seen him anywhere in the city since.

1
i stood at the corner of our condo to cross
waiting for the white man
mario looked up at me
and i met his eyes
he asked me for some change
i had none
usually i do not
something strange aroused my mind about him
my mind moved my lips
i said to him
why are you homeless
you do not look like a homeless person
he replied – i have no money
he was clean and intelligent
i could read it in his eyes
brave words that i did not know i owned left my lips
you look like a great man
that can do great things
then the white man appeared on the traffic light
he closed his eyes quietly
i left the curb with the crowd.

2
i bring mario tea
strong tea with lots of milk and sugar
i collect paper cups with caps from starbucks or blenz or other
    such places
and store them in a basket in the kitchen for mario
i bring mario tea around 2 or 3 in the afternoon
and make special trips when he sits in the rain
on the corner of seymour and pender ...

3
when i am in vancouver
i have no extra change to give mario
this has been a given from our first encounter
so instead i give him some tobacco
usually two cigarettes when i see him
during the day
he waits for them
he expects them
he saves them
he carefully tucks them away
a routine day
when i am in vancouver for a short stay

4
i brought mario a blanket once
actually two
it was late october early november and very cold
the rain began to turn to snow
i had just returned from an afternoon film
and on the corner of seymour and pender was mario asleep on the
    concrete sidewalk
i brought him soft and clean blue and pink fuzzy blankets from
    storage
and laid them down upon his large sleeping body
i felt like i was covering a small helpless child
but in reality he wasn't
the concrete sidewalk and cold falling rains was not a soft warm
    environment for any human
i left him there
i don't think he was sleeping
but his eyes remained shut

and the blankets never reappeared with mario
probably got wet and were a burden then discarded
that is all right
if only it was for the moment

5
he has his paper plate out
with very few coins on it
not that he isn't collecting a fair amount of loonies and toonies,
    nickels and dimes
and pennies from heaven

no he once told me
he gathers the excess and puts it away
and always leaves a few small coins out on the plate
waiting for his paper plate to be filled again
on the corner of seymour and pender outside the dollar pizza shops

mario doesn't necessarily eat dollar pizza slices
no
he takes his small fortune to mcdonald's
or maybe on a good day or if he has saved
he takes his coins to other places serving
steak, baked potato and salad bar

he does not drink
so he does not waste his money on wine
i know all this
because he told me so
and honoured he trusted me with this secret

mario i imagined had many secrets
many secrets we will never know

6
mario is a strange creature
he talks about jesus his savior
he talks about his tattoos on his body
he talks to himself at times perhaps when he knows you are
 looking from a distance
really do not know if it is just a show perhaps he hides behind
but he is very intelligent
you can see it in his eyes at most times (when he is not truly tired
 and worn from the streets)

sometimes he is there at the corner
sometimes he disappears

one day we were talking
most likely about nothing at all
it was early evening in late spring
and i was on my way to the drugstore to get a few things
i had given mario a few cigarettes
he carefully put them away and followed with a friendly chat
then his eyes diverted to the right down the sidewalk of pender
without moving his body or head
his eyes looked back at me
end of conversation
his eyes read
end of conversation
instructions to leave
i left and stood at the corner traffic light to cross seymour
mario did not acknowledge my departure
found this strange

i looked over and saw an average size man
mid thirties early forties
(well groomed and well dressed)
wearing a stylish brown leather jacket
he was approaching mario

as i got to the other side of the street
i turned around and saw mario pick up his things
(and in a friendly manner go with this man)

sometimes (most times) my imagination is so wild and hopeful
i believed mario to be deep undercover
working hard to etch out a living and create a better world
and maybe he is a great man destined to do great things
first impressions ... are lasting impressions
dear saint jude ... it is me again ... louise

MEDICINE BROTHER (WIND SPEAKER) I

a fleeting moment as usual
you were in my home
as i had requested
during the winter
while we were away
i asked
i prayed
for a sacred smudge
to protect and bless our home from the thievery she was
    committing
on and on as the years passed she would not stop
powerful brother you can take away her poison

in my nightly prayers i asked niscum for you to smudge and make
    holy
to lift my heavy head burdened from paranoia caused by her dark
    trickery
she comes and goes so deadly is her silence

when we returned in the mid of winter (gone five days)
cedar smoke lingered in our home
i knew you were here
but you were gone
you as always a fleeting silent unknown moment in time

wind speaker
wela'lin
i believe you believe in me
i am not crazy
you are the only one that knows
i am not what i am
i am something beyond

MEDICINE BROTHER (WIND SPEAKER) II

the loon was calling
elusive
haunting
echoes
from a distant
unknown
place in the bay

fleeting moments every spring
you arrive
call out your name
wind speaker ...
and then you are gone

HERE

here
destined to be hidden in the mist
low clouds
sweet grass fragrance swells the air from the farmers' fields
cannot find my inner voice
bipolar disorder consumes
hiding
feeling destined to being alone

rita hear my war cry it is a song
feel my drum beat it is my heart
know that i am a native daughter
my braids hang below my breast
with streaks of grey i have earned
there are no tears
defiance
i am of the first people
i am mi'kmaw
in a sea of foreign faces
oh canada
hear my song
of our native's land ...

Marie Battiste

Dr. Marie Battiste, a Mi'kmaq educator from Potlotek First Nation, Nova Scotia, is a full professor in the College of Education and Director of the Aboriginal Education Research Centre (AERC) at the University of Saskatchewan. A graduate of Harvard University (M.Ed.) and Stanford University (Ed.D.) and recipient of two honorary doctorate degrees (St. Mary's University and University of Maine at Farmington), she has published articles on cognitive imperialism, linguistic and cultural integrity, indigenous knowledge and humanities, and the decolonization of Aboriginal education. Marie has worked actively with First Nations schools as an administrator, teacher, consultant, and curriculum developer, advancing Aboriginal epistemology, languages, pedagogy, and research.

Her research interests include initiating institutional change in the decolonization of education along with the study of language and social justice policy and power. She is also involved in postcolonial educational approaches that affirm the political and cultural diversity of Canada as well as the collective healing required for transformation from colonial trauma. She is leader of a national hub at the University of Saskatchewan for the SSHRC Canadian Prevention Science Cluster aimed at identifying approaches to school-based prevention of violence and primary investigator in the SSHRC project Animating the Mi'kmaw Humanities.

She edited *Reclaiming Indigenous Voice and Vision* (UBC Press, 2000) and co-authored *Protecting Indigenous Knowledge and Heritage: A Global Challenge* with J. Youngblood Henderson (Purich Press, 2000), which received a Saskatchewan Book Award. She co-edited a special edition of the *Australian Journal of Indigenous Education* (May 2005), a special edition of *Canadian Journal of Native Education* (2010), and was senior editor for *First Nations Education in Canada: The Circle Unfolds* (UBC Press, 1995). Recipient in 2008 of the National Aboriginal Achievement Award in Education, Marie makes her home in Saskatoon, Saskatchewan, with her husband James Youngblood Henderson. She is the mother of three (Jaime, Mariah, and Annie) and grandmother of one (Jacoby).

Reflections on My Learning and Teaching as Activism and Transformation

I. Positioning my Learning

Thomas King says that stories are wondrous things, but they're dangerous. Once let loose, you can't call them back. For a large part of my speech-making life, I did not share my life stories probably for this reason. Instead, I wrote of problems I saw, issues left unresolved, analysis of theories of oppression and visioning of transformations desired in language and cultural education. I did not tell my story, my family, my life, and left it for others to do the postcolonial postmodern locations. Instead, I focused on theorizing cognitive imperialism and deconstruction of educational histories and the patterns of Eurocentrism, and the decolonizing strategies in education, drawing on my favourite Indigenous authors. But I am still learning, and in this learning I am seeking to find a better balance with my own history and what the teachings that my life experience reveals and what they have meant for the choices and paths that I have taken. Maybe this is wisdom taking its rightful place.

bell hooks offers that women from oppressed groups have stories to tell that contain so many feelings, and sharing them is an act of resistance. Speaking through stories then becomes a way to engage active self-transformation, a kind of rite of passage. My stories are not without my own versions of pain, personal and collective struggles, yet they are transforming points of learning and vectors from which I grew into new responsibilities. I try not to confuse pain with wisdom. In my current work, I am focused on how my learning spirit and the opportunities that came together as lessons learned provided for my growth and reflection, for theorizing in education and for making future changes for myself, my family, my relatives, and Indigenous peoples here and beyond. My learning spirit has been a source for my guidances that have shaped the course of my scholarship and life, much of which has not been shared widely.

Saulteaux Elder Danny Musqua has been a great inspiration for me. His sharing of the foundation for Anishenabe teachings on learning gave me a depth of understanding of the learning spirit. His stories complement my own Mi'kmaw teachings. He says that our life in the earth walk is all about learning and learning is the purpose of our life journey. At birth, spirits that have travelled with us co-join our life (after they have travelled through six other stages of development with us before arriving in the body), providing inspiration, guidance and nourishment to fulfill the purpose of the life journey. He notes that the life spirit knows what the life journey of each person is and travels with each person to offer guidance and to keep us on course. This does not happen deterministically, however, as each person's free will and desire take them in diverse paths and in each there is learning. This cosmology or theory of being is one that is repeated in ancient stories and narratives of Kluskcap, Badger, Nanabush, Wasakechuk, Raven, Napi, and others in which many diverse characters wander through life, always acquiring knowledge. In their learning, they offer ways others might benefit from that learning.

We are all on a journey to find our unique gifts given to us by the Creator. In "The Seven Fires," Elder Danny Musqua points out, "Knowledge is held by the spirits, shared by the spirits and comes from the spirits ... Our body then can be seen as carrier of the learning spirit" (D. Knight, 1999). The learning spirit then is the entity(ies) within each of us that guides our search for purpose and vision. Our special gifts (also known as inherent talents) unfold in multiple learning environments that sustain and challenge us as learners. Gregory Cajete believes such a setting enables learners to "find their heart, face and foundation" (2000). Face refers to our identity that we come to think of as ourselves, heart refers to the passion that engages our life purpose, and foundation refers to the skills needed to put our passion to work. Ultimately, all of these are connected to a spiritual source and these are essential foundations of Aboriginal learning.

My story begins in my choosing my parents, or maybe they chose me. I was born in Houlton, Maine, during potato-picking harvest, while my parents were on a brief seasonal migrant farm work stop there. They ended up staying twenty-three years before returning home to their Potlotek First Nation in Cape Breton, Nova Scotia. Twenty-three years is a long time, although I recall my mother often talking about when she would go home, the house that they would build, and the life with the relatives that return would afford. Those dreams would eventually come true for her, but why they remained in Houlton that long was a question I often wondered about. They did not stay in Maine for the great job opportunities or the wealth and prosperity it showered on us, for we started out living in a tarpaper shack behind the potato house and moved gradually into rented houses and apartments ... not quite the words to a classic country song but certainly a poignant beginning nonetheless.

Our scarcity was always a challenge, one that required my mother and father to draw on their human creativity and cultural resources to make a life. They survived by making and peddling baskets, made from ash and maple trees – beautiful colourful baskets they made from scratch which, after working for days to put together, they sold for a dollar or two each. It was a family enterprise. All of us had to learn how to make these. My dad also made axe handles, and at other times, he took work as a low-paid labourer, but that was what life was like for Indians then. When I was born, seeing our poverty, living behind the potato farm in our little one-room shack, the barren wife of the potato farmer asked my mother for me. But my mother saw no burden in her children, despite the seeming context of scarcity. However, she did let the farmer's wife name me.

Then why did they stay so long? Why would they leave the reserve, where they were assured some housing, to live in Maine and be periodically on welfare, living on the edge? Well, it was for the education that our residency promised. At the time they left the reserve, no one made it beyond early elementary school and no one went to college. Centralization in the 1940s was a federal policy that created the removal of Mi'kmaq from their traditional homelands to centralized reserves, and residential schools were still looming. My dad had a notion that my birth in the States and my brother and sisters going to school in the U.S. would assure us an education they would need to make life better for themselves in the future. So they pushed us to go to school and to do the best that we could. And despite our persistent poverty, the prejudices and racism prevalent in the town and schools, we all tried our best and when my brother, two sisters, and I had completed school, then they returned home to the reserve.

II. Language (Discourses of Difference)

We remained in the United States until I graduated from college. I was a teenager of the '60s, a time in the United States when social programming was ripe, when bilingual education was emerging as a consequence of federal initiatives trying to create improved outcomes among disadvantaged children who had little access to the curriculum due to their language and cultural backgrounds, then called "disadvantaged and culturally deprived." Martin Luther King, Jr., John F. Kennedy, feminists, and American

Indian leaders, among others, were raising the issues of equality and civil rights, human rights and Indian rights, all of which were being shaped as an emerging foundation of my social consciousness, an awareness of the plight of the poor and the effects of racism and discrimination. And it offered hope as I memorized passages from Martin Luther King's speech "I Have a Dream."

I was raised in a Mi'kmaw-speaking home, although living and growing up in Houlton, Maine, provided few opportunities for peer interaction in Mi'kmaq and there were no bilingual Mi'kmaw programs. Gradually my English got better, but my Mi'kmaw language less so, although I understood it all. Eventually I used English for most of my communication needs – a gift of colonialism, you might say, that helped me in high school and university and with my aspirations of becoming a teacher.

The '60s were characterized by a surge of civil rights, peace marches and speeches, the Viet Nam War and the American Indian Movement (AIM). My brother was in Viet Nam by then and by the time I was in college (and, in my third undergraduate year, with the help of the state's new policy to admit Maine Indians tuition free), the issues of identity and particularly Indian cultural identity were being explored, not as part of the public school curriculum, but more as pop culture. This was a time for a resurgence of cultural and racialized identity, when, as Thomas King notes, the narrow definitions of culture created an identity test of who was a real Indian. For me, I was always partly in and partly out, a status Canadian Indian, not a recognized Maine Indian (It was not until November 1991, after I left, when Mi'kmaq gained federal Indian status in Maine), an off-reserve Canadian Indian, not enough of a Mi'kmaq speaker to be considered a real Indian. Oh, what that identity test did to us! As well, there was an air of student power emerging, in protests and speeches, and many people wanted to hear about the experience of Maine Indians. Indian rights brought a new stage for the voices of American Indians.

In my last year before I graduated with my teaching degree, I was asked to give my first luncheon talk to a group of elderly women who sought to learn about the plight of the American Indian in Maine. Being asked to speak and to give voice to the varied dimensions of American Indian lives was to begin the process for critical consciousness. While I had no tools to work from, I did have models: AIM leaders, Martin Luther King, Jr., my father, who was a gregarious fellow who loved to chat with people, and my mother, who loved to tell stories. I had to develop my own voice at great risk of romanticizing or trivializing American Indians, and so I stayed safe with talking about my own people and my own stories that I knew. I admit being shaken and nervous, for it was my first time before an audience, but I did receive fifty dollars, which seemed like lots of money for a student. This would ultimately set the stage for a whole new way of being for me – raising my critical consciousness, informing my thinking, and learning about forms of activism in my study, work, and research. Certainly qualities needed for a teacher, which I eventually would become.

III. Language is Culture and Knowledge

In the late 1970s, after the federal policy of Indian Control of Indian Education had been passed, my own community of Chapel Island in Nova Scotia was developing plans to assume control over its schools. In the years before it did, I had helped lay the foundation with my home band, writing drafts of the vision that I thought should unfold in language and cultural education. But I was in California beginning my doctorate degree, and they began with an all-Anglo staff, which at first helped to develop the basics of education but had little effect on the language and cultural part of students' education. Assimilation was well on its projected path. So after I completed my degree in 1983, I was asked to return to make my earlier vision a reality with the first Mi'kmaw graduates of the Teacher Education Program (TEP) at the Mi'kmaq-Maliseet Institute (MMI) at the University of New Brunswick in Fredericton.

Hiring an all-Mi'kmaw staff at Mi'kmawey School in Chapel Island, we set out to create the first bilingual education school in the Maritimes. We had early resistances among some parents who felt that the band school could not compete with public schooling, but as education director, I pursued with a passion a Mi'kmaw school with Mi'kmaw-speaking teachers, a curriculum based on Mi'kmaw knowledge, hieroglyphics, Mi'kmaw historical knowledge, Mi'kmaq traditional governance, spirituality, and oral traditions. The 1980s brought new foundations for language and cultural pride, and the community responded positively to these developments. Elders offered guidance and support, and helped in every way they could, and in turn I found every way possible to keep them involved in how our school shaped a community consciousness in multiple community events. We were the hub of the Chapel Island community.

While administering the school on a small budget was challenging, we found lots of ways to show others what we were doing. My teachers and I travelled long distances each day from one reserve to another, and in our many relationships, other communities began to hear of our successes, our language and cultural programming and they wanted to be part of that. I used the media often to share our school activities and the coverage was shown throughout Cape Breton. It created a lot of talk.

Several parents sought to have their local school boards approve buses to transport their children to our school. While that did not happen, what it did do was politicize parents to want a different kind of education for their children, the kind we had to offer, and they then pressured their school boards to find buses to take their children to our school or to have them develop an education like ours. In so doing, our experiment with Mi'kmawey School in Potlotek First Nation to pursue a commitment to Mi'kmaq language and cultural education transformed First Nations schools in Cape Breton, and later in mainland Nova Scotia, toward language and cultural learning and stirred a renewed sense of pride and ownership. Thereafter, all the band schools turned to an education modelled on language and cultural programming.

The people who were feeling the dreaded assimilation push now felt ready to assist in making different outcomes built on their languages and cultures. Today Mi'kmaw Kina'matnewey is the only legislated First Nations educational authority for nine Mi'kmaw communities in Nova Scotia. They continue to operate an educational authority drawing on the shared resources among these communities to deliver quality education for Mi'kmaw communities.

IV. Indigenous Knowledge Requires Protection

In the '80s and into the '90s, the Grand Keptin of the Mi'kmaw Nation took a complaint against Canada to the United Nations. Their self-determination was being affected by the federal government's lack of consultation with them on constitutional reform. This contravened the provisions of self-determination as found in the International Covenant of Civil and Political Rights, which Canada signed in 1976. This action, which spanned at least a decade, brought many of us to Geneva and to the Working Group on Indigenous Populations (WGIP).

At that time, my husband and I met Indigenous leaders around the world and together we conceptualized the strategy for Indigenous knowledge and began the Indigenous renaissance in all sectors of the U.N. One of our friends was a Greek woman, Dr. Erica Daes, who was the chairperson for the Working Group on Indigenous Populations. She asked us to take on a research project to address Indigenous knowledge and develop some principles and guidelines for the protection of Indigenous heritage. In 1993, we completed this work with a draft document that would take us through consultations throughout the Indigenous world to their completion in 2000 when these were ratified by the WGIP. This work in examining the Indigenous intellectual and cultural property rights in Canada, the United States, and beyond, led to our book in 2000, *Protecting Indigenous Knowledge and Heritage: A Global Challenge*.

In 1999, we took these protection principles and the issues to the Grand Council of Mi'kmaq and asked they consider the implications for the protection of Mi'kmaw knowledge and peoples, given the appropriation and exploitation of Indigenous peoples' knowledge that was occurring globally. The Grand Council then directed the Grand Keptin Alex Denny to appoint a volunteer committee of elders, leaders, teachers, and others to make recommendations regarding the protection issues and to report back the following year to the Grand Council.

I was made part of that committee and after a year of meetings, research and deliberations, we arrived at our own Ethics Principles and Guidelines which was recommended to the Grand Council. A committee was then assigned the work, which they called the Mi'kmaq Eskimuapimk, or the Mi'kmaw Ethics Watch, which has been operating since, with a volunteer group from our communities who reviews all research that is done in our territories.

The Mi'kmaw Ethics Watch has since served to inspire other communities, throughout Canada and beyond, to do the same in developing their own self-determining research ethics. It is an example of self-governance at its best. These Ethics Watch Principles can be accessed at the Cape Breton University website in the Mi'kmaq Research College Institute.

V. Postcolonial Voices

In 1993, after fifteen years in Nova Scotia reserves, my family moved to Saskatoon, Saskatchewan, as my husband and I joined the faculty of the University of Saskatchewan. As starting faculty, I was challenged to think about what my research program was going to be. I was still pondering this when we learned of the request for proposals for the last of the SSHRC (Social Sciences and

Humanities Research Council) Summer Institutes. So we put together a proposal to bring postcolonial scholars to campus to address the theme Cultural Restoration of Oppressed Indigenous Peoples.

That proposal was successful, and I was asked to be the Coordinator for this institute, a job that seemed insurmountable, having to prepare for an international ten-day gathering of Indigenous and non-Indigenous scholars. A year of planning finally brought together these scholars, many of whom I had only met there, but with whom I remain lasting friends today – Leroy Littlebear, Gregory Cajete, Graham and Linda Smith, Linda Hogan, Eduardo Duran, Len Findlay, and many others.

If I thought that was an impossible task, it was only the beginning, as I next had to put the proceedings of this gathering together in a report to SSHRC and then to compile the edited book, *Reclaiming Indigenous Voice and Vision*. The completion of that book would occur during my first sabbatical year, providing the intellectual framework of the Indigenous renaissance based on Indigenous languages. When I put together my sabbatical proposal that year, I was advised that I should not say I wanted to produce a book. Anything could interrupt a sabbatical, I was told, and I should seek modest goals. Just say a book outline and at most, a chapter. So I did. That year, I had two of my books published – a month apart just before the conclusion of my leave, a very productive sabbatical year at that.

VI. Indigenous Science, Humanities and Learning

At the turn of the century, Indigenous Knowledge was a term being used with increasing frequency. Before that, culture was the operative word. Once we had defined that term in *Protecting Indigenous Knowledge and Heritage*, it became clear what was most unclear was why Indigenous Knowledge, as a distinct knowledge system from Eurocentrism, was being ignored on one hand and appropriated for market gain on the other. For example, there are two disciplinary areas which usually did not have "Indigenous" attached to them at all: science and humanities.

Social scientists had long developed their disciplinary knowledge on the cultures/knowledge of Indigenous peoples, attempting to discover the exotic aspects of Indigenous cultures in the disciplines of anthropology and linguistics. We were aware of how more recently scientists supported by corporations and multinationals had begun to see how these once-thought primitive and exotic cultures could become instrumental to their economic and social political growth. Particularly, Indigenous peoples' knowledge of plant and animal behaviour, as well as of their self-management of natural resources, had inspired a new burgeoning field of involvement and interest among researchers and academicians worldwide.

This interest has been the thrust of a new hot button issue dealing with Indigenous knowledge and intellectual and cultural property that has fuelled a political confrontation of Indigenous and non-Indigenous peoples. Once again a new form of global racism threatened Indigenous peoples, a racism in which cultural capital is used as a form of superiority over colonized peoples.

As a board member of an international development agency, I was once asked to review projects in Ecuador and Guatemala. In one visit we went from one building to the next at the University of Guatemala, looking at the ten million dollar machine that did one thing and a forty million dollar machine that did another, for these machines were bought by Japan and Germany, showcasing how the essences of plants were extracted and packaged for commercial production. I asked how they learned of these plants, and they told me about the local women who were interviewed – "wives' knowledge," they called Indigenous knowledge – and how the researchers did interviews among them for this information. What did the local women get in return? I asked. I thought surely some portion of these millions. No, they got a journal in an accessible language. This is the kind of ethics of science that needed to be opened up.

So in a series of yearly dialogues over a ten-year period, we participated with Leroy Littlebear and other Indigenous scholars and elders, together with non-Indigenous scientists to discuss the various perspectives of science and the issues that have been raised about appropriation. It was fascinating stuff, and some meetings were headier than others, especially how quantum physics and Indigenous ways of knowing were merging. But in all the instances, the Indigenous scholars provided enough material to make this dialogue compelling to non-Indigenous scientists, many of whom were part of the Fetzer Institute in Kalamazoo, Michigan, including the late David Bohm. He was particularly intrigued, for he had noted how inadequate the English language was for explaining quantum physics and how Indigenous languages could create new words on the spot to explain events in the processs of happening. The verb-based languages were far more capable of explaining the processes unfolding in the animate world than English was.

These dialogues are continuing, and Indigenous knowledge (IK) and the sciences and ecologies are still very much a conversation emerging, although there are now more readily found institutions that are examining the issues of IK and their ethics, including UNESCO, the Convention on Biodiversity, the Canadian secretariat for the Convention, Heritage Canada, the Departments of Forestry, Parks Canada, Agriculture, Indian Affairs, and many more areas. For obvious reasons, the ethics issues need to remain on the front burners and my work remains in that area.

The second foundation of IK was Indigenous humanities. I remember once receiving a conference brochure for an international conference on humanities, at Harvard I think, which covered the humanities of the world: Asia, India, Europe, but there was no Indigenous humanities or at least not of Indigenous peoples, regardless of place. This seemed like a major gap. Did we not have history, art, literature, fine arts, performance and drama, and philosophy which humanities as a global term did cover? Yet why were these areas always Eurocentric or Euro-Asian humanities and not any other continents?

Indigenous humanities was a much broader concept than the historical focus of Native Studies and in my mind needed to be acknowledged, including those Indigenous humanities models like Buffy Sainte-Marie. Her extraordinary gifts have been used to serve not narrow personal interests but instead to benefit her traditions, her ever extending communities, and those she touches and enriches as an exemplary citizen, as a universal soldier and as a Changing Woman for creativity and justice. (Changing Woman is a mythological and metaphorical term used in Navajo teachings of the Creation Story to understand the changing flux of the earth and its life-giving and life-sustaining capacities. In Navajo teachings, change is active and feminine.)

In 2005, Dr. Cathryn McConaghy and I were asked to co-edit a special issue of the *Australian Journal of Indigenous Education* and this was a place to put our theme to work: "Thinking Place: Animating the Indigenous Humanities." To understand Indigenous humanities, we wrote, was first to understand the exclusions of Indigenous knowledge in the context of education and to understand why education had not served the interests of Indigenous peoples.

In "Indigenous Knowledge: The Metaphor of Indigenous Education," Tewa educator Gregory Cajete offered the metaphor of the split mind, /pin geh heh/, meaning not being of a whole mind, having a split head, which describes how many Indigenous students have had to endure a seemingly schizophrenic life of being an Indigenous person trying to live with Indigenous knowledge, language, and sensitivities within a hostile Eurocentric society. This split head consciousness is not a peculiar individual affliction but rather a larger consciousness that is revealed in multiple forms among Aboriginal peoples as they navigate through the conventional educational systems. This split head consciousness is an educational outcome that arises from a denied consciousness, heritage and humanity of Aboriginal children and their descendents, but also has been the source of inequity, exclusion, and domination over Indigenous peoples worldwide.

Education remains one of the critical sites for postcolonial antiracism work, particularly since the modern structures of the economic and education systems have been crafted out of Eurocentrism. Eurocentrism is our challenge, as it has created our educational failures. Eurocentrism is not defined as a cultural attribute of any one group but characterizes a way of knowing, thinking, scholarship, and so on where there is a centre and a periphery and from which by a force of diffusionism the centre gives to the periphery all its knowledge, laws, education, and assumptions of good and bad. It is a kind of one-way street based on a notion of superiority. As a result, the purposes and structures of education and its languages have not been politically neutral or devoid of politics as they are also sustained by public policy and funds. It is important to understand that in Canada, as is found elsewhere, every political decision about society and its past and its future have been addressed without the input and direction of Indigenous knowledge and people. Taking IK from Indigenous students and replacing it with Eurocentrism is what I have called cognitive imperialism.

Indigenous peoples have not participated in Canada's political creation, its socio-cultural transformations, and its goal setting. If it were not that the Indigenous peoples of the world have held the land, and were the original creators of potatoes, rice, corn, the staples of the global food chain and are caring for eighty percent of the biodiversity of the world, Indigenous peoples would be minor players in all of its configurations.

Today, the critically important postcolonial quest for Indigenous peoples is to bring their knowledge and practices fully into their children's lives. Reclaiming, recovering, restoring, and renewing Indigenous peoples' rights, which include IK and languages, is a revisionist educational project of great magnitude. It is clearly a project that many Indigenous peoples have taken to all their sites of work and study, whether in the political activism of blockades on the roads, in protests in and over the waters, in the courts, and in schools and classrooms. And teachers and students everywhere need to be aware of its significance.

VII. Developing Indigenous Rights

The United Nations has long supported this work and after more than two decades, on September 17, 2007, the Declaration of the Rights of Indigenous Peoples was ratified. While 143 countries of the world agreed, Canada and three other countries opposed, Canada on the grounds that the Declaration conflicted with the nation's constitution. However, Canada officially endorsed the Declaration in November 2010. (Australia had ratified it in April 2009, New Zealand in April 2010. In December 2010, President Barack Obama stated the U.S. would.) In the Declaration are the standards that need to be fully adopted and pursued to create equal rights with all other citizens. Allow me to offer just a small glimpse at those provisions, especially those related to education:

Article 14
1. Indigenous peoples have the right to establish and control their educational systems and institutions providing education in their own languages, in a manner appropriate to their cultural methods of teaching and learning.
2. Indigenous individuals, particularly children, have the right to all levels and forms of education of the State without discrimination.
3. States shall, in conjunction with indigenous peoples, take effective measures, in order for indigenous individuals, particularly children, including those living outside their communities, to have access, when possible, to an education in their own culture and provided in their own language.

Article 15
1. Indigenous peoples have the right to the dignity and diversity of their cultures, traditions, histories and aspirations which shall be appropriately reflected in education and public information.
2. States shall take effective measures, in consultation and cooperation with the indigenous peoples concerned, to combat prejudice and eliminate discrimination and to promote tolerance, understanding and good relations among indigenous peoples and all other segments of society.

The implementation of these rights is not just a nation's legislative and policy responsibility. It will take every citizen and every institution to ensure that these rights have a place in the fashioning of society and its institutions. This work is unfolding in Canada in multiple sites, especially the Prairies.

In 2005 and again in 2009, the University of Saskatchewan College of Education prioritized Aboriginal education in their first and second Integrated Plan, continuing to expand upon the Aboriginal Foundation Document. The university solidified its commitment by creating a centre aimed at building partnerships to sustain Aboriginal education research and enriching opportunities for graduate and undergraduate students: to explore theory and promising practices, and to address issues raised by Aboriginal learners in the schools. I became the first academic director of the new Aboriginal Education Research Centre (AERC). This centre supports the University of Saskatchewan's Aboriginal Foundation Document that positions Aboriginal education and students as priorities to achieve improved outcomes for them and to ensure that every unit in the university will find support for their Aboriginal initiatives.

In the first year of the centre, AERC applied for and was invited by the Canadian Council on Learning (CCL) to co-lead the national Aboriginal Learning Knowledge Centre in partnership with the First Nations Adult and Higher Education Consortium in Calgary. Our mandate was to create knowledge exchange in the area of Aboriginal learning, and thereby to improve the conditions and practices in education and non-formal learning that impact on Aboriginal learners and their successes.

With six thematic areas called bundles, and a consortium of over one hundred partners, we were funded by the CCL to share knowledge to improve learning in many areas of Aboriginal lifelong learning: Learning from Place, Nourishing the Learning Spirit, Aboriginal Languages, Diverse Systems of Learning, Pedagogy of Professions, and Technology and Learning. With crosscutting themes in literacy, gender, francophone minority communities, e-literacy, and culture, we are seeking to normalize Indigenous knowledge in the content and delivery of education in all schools and, institutions, where not just Aboriginal learners are present but for all learners, and to share promising practices and sustain the dialogue of improvement and change in all areas of learning.

I led Nourishing the Learning Spirit, which focused on the effect holistic learning has on learners, helping them to connect more meaningfully with their own spiritual selves and to draw more meaningfully on their learning spirit. Holistic learning has both deepened and raised my own spirituality. In addition, it has created new relationships with scholars and communities, and built new alliances to work in partnerships that address the educational outcomes and gaps among Aboriginal learners. Our work continues in multiple sites and activities with many organizations across Canada, and our most recent shared outcomes have been in developing holistic models for identifying learning in communities.

VIII. Conclusion

Elders have helped me to see these lifetime opportunities to grow are part of the emergence of myself as a learner responding to the guidances of my learning spirit. My learning path has been a winding road of many unexpected surprises and new forms of critical consciousness, resistance, activism, and transformation. It is interesting how a life unfolds ... In an interview in Saskatoon's *The*

StarPhoenix in 2007, Inuit singer Susan Aglukark remarked that when she left home in 1991 to be an Inuit translator for the federal government, the last thing on her mind was the thing she ended up doing, singing worldwide. "It found me, rather than I found it," she said. This is the nature of the learning spirit. It too has found me and in so doing has helped me to build my own capacities and to share them more in multiple areas to work on my own responsibilities and perhaps to stimulate change, and to be open to new possibilities for my growth in learning. This arrives as wisdom at its best. I share these reflections on my life experiences to honour my own learning spirits and to help others to reflect on their own journeys as their ideas and work take root in social justice, equity, and transformation of all learners. This is the tradition left behind by Elder Rita Joe for whom this publication is dedicated. She has been a role model and an inspiration. Wela'liek.

References

Cajete, G. (2000). Indigenous knowledge: The Pueblo metaphor of Indigenous education. In M. Battiste (Ed.), *Reclaiming Indigenous voice and vision* (pp. 192-208). Vancouver: University of British Columbia Press.

Connection to Culture. (2007, March 26). *The StarPhoenix*. Retrieved July 5, 2011, from http://www.canada.com

Knight, D. (1999). The seven fires: The lifelong process of growth and learning as explained by Saulteaux Elder Danny Musqua. Masters of Education Project, Department of Educational Foundations, University of Saskatchewan, Saskatoon.

Peter C. Julian

Peter Julian currently resides in Paqtnkek, Nova Scotia, with his two beautiful children and his wonderful wife. He is a former student of the Transition Year Program at Dalhousie University. He is presently working on his B.A. in Anthropology at Saint Francis Xavier University in Antigonish, Nova Scotia.

Peter began writing at an early age to help him cope with many of his thoughts and emotions. As well as writing poetry, he also enjoys reading it. His favourite poet is Emily Dickinson.

Poem 1

You wanna hate me
For what I am
You wanna take from me
And do not want to hear my objections
You treat me with no
Respect
And you expect me to listen
Do you feel the frustration
Building inside
That begs to be set free
For both our sakes
Stop
I am not old
Nor
Am I wise
I do not know better
I am naïve
I am what it is you
Believe me to be
What you think of me
Is reflected in your actions
How I feel is reflected in mine
I am not dumb
I am not savage
I am
I exist
I am the product of
Generations
Of oppression incompetence ... wardship
Now I am here and you are there
Tell me now
what it is you think of me
and I shall do the same

Poem 2

the loser befriends himself
again and again
opportunity passes him by
sadly
he watches
asking himself why it is like this
independent
or
reclusive
do they not understand me
do I understand myself
shadows of what was once
a childhood so full of hope
is now a dark hallway in one
lonely direction
and I am in it with no end in sight
society's cold touch
has avoided me
what is it that they fear
over this keyboard
through this keyboard
I scream all of my frustrations
Loudly
Violently
unanswered and unconcerned
are those who do not listen
anyway
incoherent become my thoughts
as the fingers feel the keys
gliding over them
they sort of tickle
and tease
is this what human contact is like

funny
are you still there
or did you go
I understand
I think
Why does the sadness
last so long
Why
is it so efficient
my morale lacks any conviction
so what continues to move my feet
sheer will
to not die here I suppose
the scenery is less than exquisite

Poem 3

what is poetry
am I constructing it now
if I hit these keys
will someday a person
read it and wonder
who I was
and why so much time I spent
writing all of this
asking myself
doubting myself
torturing myself
condemning myself
will my thoughts so full of vanity
intrigue you
will you become inspired
or be filled with disgust
self-absorbed
but life is a gift
like a fifty-dollar bill
precious to some
disposable to others
is it okay
if I think what I might
stay if you will
but just watch and listen to see
if my meaning comes
somehow I keep
missing it

Poem 4

A
glowing darkness
primes itself
absence of fear worries
me
acceptance
or
hopelessness
each prepare me
pawing through the dark
trying to feel the light
a
cool breeze
warms me
glides over my skin
like a faithful whisper
but it has no voice
the blackness
blinds me
like my heart
my eyes are useless
forgive me

Poem 5

opposed
facing the
un-face-able
the complete
emptiness behind me
sends sensations of
déjà vu
anxiety
like after a day of drinking
shaking
but not so much afraid
but rather
uninformed, full of uncertainty
as to why you have come here
to oppose me
you take without asking
without consideration
your appetite
is insatiable
I am not an easy task
I fear nothing
Death, is it your time
Will you walk in the fields with me?

Poem 6

a man and his son
a man
a time for growth
a time to learn
a time for
tyranny
regime of sadistic rule
an iron fist that
makes me bow
I am yours
and you are my master
I am but no more than six
responsibility begins at three
you foster a growth, a hell spawn of hate
born into the bondage
of anger
it grows and it blackens
all that is pure
force to face it the rest of
my existence
trace it back to you
now, an old man
full of fear
powerless
do I take what you have denied me
do I let myself succumb
to what has enslaved you
never
for you are weak
and I am strong
I am
your son
your legacy

will be
in my hands
but fear not, for on that day
when all that is wrong in me
perishes with you
I shall leave it there
your legacy,
with you

SMA'KNIS

Destiny a warrior meets
Another proud mother weeps
Devotion of sons and daughters
Sacrifices of mothers and fathers
Blood runs thick as belief runs thin
Only those who are dead and done fighting are the ones who win
Where and why is it them we are sending
And how is it way over there it is us they're defending
To what cost is it finally enough
And when will the survivors have suffered enough
The belief to do what is expected
Is why them I have always respected
Even after so much loss and so many taken
My belief in what's right was never shaken
So those who can still listen but have marched off into the night
To those who have sent them will you whisper then "It was right"

Not quite day, not quite night

The floor is so cold, the bed so hard
Everything that I knew is now so far
The lack of necessities makes me weak
Why is it so evil every time that I speak
Everything that is good lies under the steeple
And everything that is wrong, they tell me, lies with my people
They tell me to forget everything that I know
Then, they say, God won't hate me so
They beat me when I speak, they beat me when they catch me
    praying
They beat me so much I can't hear what they're saying
It hurts when I sit, it hurts when I stand
It hurts to be native; it hurts to be who I am
They open my skin, with their medicine made of leather
My friend can no longer walk right, but they say he's now better
He now prays to the cross, he speaks their talk
He can no longer run, so to heaven he'll have to walk
They say our people are the devil in disguise
But my parents love me, why would they teach me lies
I am no longer native, but I am still not white
I am like dusk or dawn, not quite day, not quite night

To my granddad
Forever, my love and respect

The Letter

I think this time too long I've been gone
I don't think she's right I don't think I'm wrong
Was I wrong to cause her pain
Was it her fault she knew my name
Could things be worse, could they get better
Are her explanations in that letter
Will she tell me that she tried
Will she tell me it was my fault she lied
Are there truths that leave that twisted tongue
Are we really that naïve when we're young
Will she say how I caused her all this hurt
Will she describe the fruitlessness of all our hard work
Is there a reason I should be believing
That this day would never come, that she would be up and leaving
My heart's heavy with all the right or wrong reasons
I gave up my heart, but one of us has broken it
I hold the letter in my hand and I dare not open it
I light my cigarette, gaze at the flame
It was always cute how she wrote my name
So many things I've lost, so many things I shoulda learned
So many questions go unanswered as I watch the letter burn
The sorrow, regret in the smoke I can taste
The heat from the fire dries the tears on my face
I butt out my cigarette as five minutes passes
I look down and wonder, is my heart among those ashes

My reservation

Have you ever felt the scorn of racism
I feel it every day
I try to explain to the non-believers
But alternate explanations are given in an attempt
To drive my suspicions away
But if it were all that simple
Then why do I feel like this after every long day
Instead of learning at school I come away always feeling this way
What did I ever do to you that was so wrong
For you to look and act like this to me
I've taken nothing from you and yet every day your country
    benefits from me
You've taken my land, my language, my culture
You even almost took my faith
That people are capable of good things
If you've only listened to what they had to say
My whole life I've felt like I've been at odds
Trying my best to just assimilate
But whenever I feel like I've gotten close
My life has created enough experiences to the point where I can't
    relate
There are very few non-natives who could truly appreciate our
    situation
I go to your town everyday, but how often do you come to my
    reservation

GRATEFUL

Anger, suicide, drugs and alcohol
So many ways a native can fall
Class of 2002 more incarcerated
Than there are graduated
No more warriors, no more chiefs
Just lost children who share
Problems instead of beliefs
The Resi fresh on the crippled minds
So they buy silence with nickels and dimes
Will compensation re-teach the language
Will compensation deliver us from the anguish
Not allowed to no longer speak of the sins committed against them
So I'll compensate and speak for them
The cycle of violence is deeper than most would like to believe
And in the Resi is where they planted the seed
Can you hear the children crying so young taken from their homes
Beaten until they're socially awkward and writing depressing poems
The survivors are strong many resisted the change
But even though they were still "Indian" they weren't the same
Allowed to finally return home with the new-found education
Incapable of showing love creates another crippled generation
Discipline replaces once-taught lessons
And today I'm told to count my blessings
Thank God and the government for letting me exist
I don't know where I'd be without all this blissfulness

Robert Bernard

James "Robert" Bernard is the son of Charles J. and Rose Bernard of We'koqma'q Mi'kmaw First Nation community. When Robert was thirteen, Charlie J. (Soln in Mi'kmaw), the older brother of Rita (Bernard) Joe, passed away. Robert's ten siblings helped to ensure he was raised with many strong values such as respecting elders and staying close to family. Robert learned these values well and keeps them as a foundation for his everyday life. He now still lives and works in the community, with his wife Kelly (Walker, of Hay's River, Nova Scotia) and their four children: Jordan, Kaylyn, Kassidy, and Karmin. He composed his poem "I am free now, let me go" upon the death of his aunt and it was read at her funeral. Robert's aunt Rita Joe always encouraged him to write and share his works and he plans on writing a book of poetry himself.

A natural talent for fast-pitch softball enabled Robert to travel across Canada and the U.S.A. from an early age, which allowed him to learn about different cultures. Today, sport still plays a pivotal role in his life: Robert volunteers many hours to coach youth in several different sports such as hockey, softball, basketball, and badminton. From 1997 to 2007 he was the Executive Director of Nova Scotia's first Aboriginal Sport and Recreation organization dedicated to the advancement of youth participation in organized sport and recreation activities. He also owns Diversity Management Group (DMG), an Aboriginal consulting firm that delivers capacity development contracts for governments and industry focusing on creating opportunities for Aboriginal businesses and communities across Atlantic Canada. For the future, Robert's interests include developing stronger ways to enhance governance and economic development models in First Nation communities for the long-term benefit of families and youth populations. He is also very interested in developing an Aboriginal role model program that would allow young children and youth the benefit of accessing positive and structural guidance from accomplished and experienced community volunteers of all ages.

Rita Joe, The Mi'kmaw Poet

A small girl sat quietly all alone
Wondering what all the fuss was about
Her mom had just passed away
Through the birth of a sibling
Two gone and a future in doubt

She was lost in a confusing world
A child without her mother
The circle of life that circled too soon
A child who would never forget this day
A hurt that would forever flow

And now she was leaving home
To attend Residential School
A long ride, then many children
The feeling of emptiness
Circling deep within her

So many faces, so much sadness
She wanted to go home
She didn't understand
And all she ever wanted
Was someone to hold her hand

Children torn from their parents
So much culture and tradition lost
A language bent but not broken
A legacy many families suffer today
The helpless who became strong

She wondered about the reasons why
She would learn about it someday
Who would do this to a little child
On our own land, in front of our families?
Imagine if that happened today

And as the days went by
She worked very hard
She knew the time would come
When she would be out the door
To find freedom and a new life

She would run away to the USA
So very determined to survive
She would meet a young man there
And soon a new baby and a move back home
A growing family, exactly where she wanted to be

Before long the years went by
She started to write about our people
At first a simple phrase and then some more
Then she turned these words into a book or two
Then three, four and more and more

She wrote about her life
And the things we cherish as Lnu
How the outside world turns our way
To see the gifts of our people
As understanding grows

Because of her words
People are now coming to know
The many barriers we climb
The legacies we are left with
As we take the next step forward

It is true that throughout her days
Her thoughts remained strong
Her purpose always driving the messages
The little girl, the warrior woman
We all came to know

She accomplished great things
In the lifetime she was blessed to have
And now the pages of history
Will bear her name
Rita Joe, the Mi'kmaw Poet

ROBERT BERNARD

I AM THINKING OF YOU

My Auntie, I am sitting here thinking of you
How much you must have been through in this world
How much you have accomplished
The words you have written on paper

You have helped our people
To understand where we have been
And to learn about the things that we have been through
How badly we were treated by those who we thought were our
    friends
And how badly we have treated ourselves

I think about how many you have lost in this world
How young you were when you lost your parents
And how your brothers gradually left you
How much we loved them, yet we couldn't stop them from going

Then your husband, when he was taken home too
I know that in your heart, he took a lot of you with him
Now, I think of you and how strong you keep going
How you keep being beautiful, how you keep helping
Even though the days keep getting harder

How your family must love you
And how they must be so proud of you
Because you keep going so strong
Even today

My Auntie, I just want to tell you
That we love you too
The only thing I regret
Is that we didn't know each other more

I have children now,
And I read to them about this woman, Rita Joe
And I tell them stories and say to them,
"This is your Auntie." And they sit in wonder
And smile

I AM FREE NOW, LET ME GO

Take a deep breath
And close your eyes now
Gently rest your head back
I am in a calm place.

Can you see me? How happy I am?
I am smiling, dancing and singing
I am free again
No more pain.

The sun has shone for me today,
My arms stretching out to feel the warmth
No more limitations
Only happiness
My purpose served.

I have lived in you and you in me
I must go to a new place now
To fly away in the spirit world
With the ones we love.

It's been a while since I've seen my family
The ones who have gone before me
At first I am almost amazed that I am here
And finally as I take their hands in mine
I know that I am home now.

Many years ago as a child
The world was so cold
I wondered how we could live
So much hurt and fear
They did not understand our way.

Many a leaf has fallen
With hearts and minds challenged
About who we are
It is not over – there is more to come
Take your place in time.

You are my kin, my family
Ni'kmaq, we are of the same blood
Look around you
The connection is there
In you lie the pieces of a puzzle.
And now I leave this world
Full of love for me
I am happy – Wel'tasi
I am smiling
Because of you

I am free now, let me go.

Daniel N. Paul

Born on the Shubenacadie Indian Reserve in Hants County, Daniel Paul is a member of the Mi'kmaq First Nation and registered with the Millbrook Band in Truro, Nova Scotia. For more than thirty years, he has worked as an author, journalist, consultant, and volunteer to eradicate racism. The residents of Nova Scotia, the Nova Scotia Human Rights Commission, the Micmac Native Friendship Centre, The Confederacy of Mainland Mi'kmaq and many others have benefitted from his consensus-building skills and commitment to the community. Through his newspaper columns and his book *We Were Not the Savages*, now in its third edition, he has helped to restore the proud heritage and history of the Mi'kmaq nation.

He is the recipient of many awards in recognition of his outstanding contributions to the Mi'kmaq community and to Nova Scotia as a whole. In 1997, he received an honorary Doctor of Letters degree from Université de Sainte Anne in Church Point, Nova Scotia. He was named to the Order of Nova Scotia in 2002 and the Order of Canada in 2005. In 2007, he received the Grand Chief Donald Marshall Sr. Memorial Award. Most recently, in June 2011, the Nova Scotia Community College awarded him an honorary diploma in recognition of a lifetime of promoting human rights.

However, his most appreciated honours are the dozens of letters, mugs, eagle feathers, and other items given to him by students as thanks for helping them better understand the importance of according all peoples human dignity and respect.

To learn more about Daniel Paul, visit his website at www.danielnpaul.com.

Honouring Rita

Indians have in the past been portrayed as the bad guys. I write the positive image of my people, the Mi'kmaq. – Rita Joe

Rita Joe, a Mi'kmaq Indian, was born in Whycocomagh, Nova Scotia, in 1932, daughter of Josie and Annie Bernard. She met Frank Joe in Boston, Massachusetts; they married and moved to Eskasoni, Cape Breton, Nova Scotia. They raised eight of their own children and adopted two boys.

Rita Joe started writing in 1973. She wrote to the *Micmac News*, a Cape Breton newsletter, periodically. One section of the newsletter included poems and stories. Little did Rita Joe know that her poems in the future would be internationally acclaimed. The editor of the newsletter gave her some very good advice: "Save your poems and don't throw them away." Over time, she penned and saved, then shared her poetry.

Her first book, *Poems of Rita Joe*, was published in 1978. Her second book, *Song of Eskasoni*, was released in 1988. Three years later, in 1991, she published her third book, *Lnu And Indians We're Called*. In 1994, her work – poetry and a short autobiography – was included in *Kelusultiek: Original Women's Voices of Atlantic Canada*. Kelusultiek means "we speak" and was a compilation of poems and stories. Her memoir *Song of Rita Joe: Autobiography of a Mi'kmaq Poet* was published in 1996. In 1997, she co-edited *The Mi'kmaq Anthology* with Lesley Choyce. *We Are the Dreamers: recent and early poetry* appeared in 1999. Breton Books published her final book, *For the Children*, posthumously in 2008.

Rita was named to the Order of Canada on October 23, 1989. She was invested in the Order on April 18, 1990. The following is the press release issued upon her appointment:

> A Micmac poet, she is proud of her native heritage which she shares through her books, notably *Poems of Rita Joe* and *Song of Eskasoni*. As an active member of the Nova Scotia Writers' Federation, and a speaker at numerous engagements, she has been a true ambassador for her people, promoting native art and culture across Canada and in the United States.

Rita herself said in *We Are the Dreamers*, "I was only a housewife with a dream to bring laughter to the sad eyes of my people and trusting the anchor we live by to complete the woven tale we are still telling."

On March 20, 2007, the Great Spirit welcomed a wonderful person home to the Land of Souls, His daughter Rita. She left a great legacy of written poetic works for our Mi'kmaq nation to treasure — her words of wisdom, expressed in her poetry, will resonate throughout the ages. She joins her late husband Frank, who also inspired others with his accomplishments later in life.

In fact, it was through Frank, who I met back in the 1970s when I was employed by Indian Affairs, that I met Rita. Frank, like most of us born prior to the 1940s, did not have much of a formal education. However, in mid-life he got his act together and remedied his lack of a formal education by doing the necessary preparatory work to enter university, graduating with a teacher's licence, and then getting a teaching job. To say the least, I was very impressed, and congratulated him profoundly.

From 1993 to 2004, while I was still writing for the Halifax *Chronicle Herald*, I wanted to write a column about Rita and her family. It was around 1995, at an arts and crafts show at the Halifax Metro Centre, that I first discussed it with her. We agreed to do it when our busy schedules would permit. In the final analysis, it never got done. This wasn't because of procrastination on our parts but simply because our schedules just didn't click. After a while, we kind of got a kick out of the failed effort.

After reading my book *We Were Not the Savages*, Rita congratulated me for putting into writing for posterity the suffering that the Mi'kmaq suffered at the hands of the British colonials and, after Confederation, Canadian governments. She said that I had delivered "a powerful message." Her words of praise and appreciation for something that took over ten years of my life to finish were music to my ears. I shall continue to savour them for the rest of my days.

She asked me at that time if I hated the English for the harm they had done our people. I told her no, I just hated the fact that even in modern times they still would not own up to the evils some of their ancestors had perpetrated and make amends. I asked her the same question and her response was, "I don't hate anyone. It does no good to hate."

Rita's works project the insights of a gentle but strong soul. They are a gift from her for generations to enjoy for lifetimes. Let's use them wisely to refresh our minds when we hurt. These words she left in an unfinished poem say it best: "On the day I am blue, I go again to the wood where the tree is swaying, arms touching you like a friend, and the sound of the wind so alone like I am; whispers here, whispers there, come and just be my friend."

May Rita enjoy peace and tranquillity with the Great Spirit in the Land of Souls for eternity. She lived her life with dignity and respect for others and, as her story reveals, she did it extremely well.

My Story

I was born December 5, 1938, in a small log cabin on Shubenacadie Indian Reserve (now Indian Brook), Nova Scotia, to Sarah Agnes (Noel) and William Gabriel Paul. I'm the twelfth of their fourteen children. I reside in Halifax in semi-retirement with my wife, Patricia. We have two daughters, Lenore and Cerena, and two granddaughters, Jenna and Julia.

My place of birth was preordained three years prior to my birth by a blatant act of racism committed against my family by Anglo Caucasian society. Until the fall of 1935, my father worked on the Saint John, New Brunswick, waterfront as a stevedore. Consequently, he was a taxpayer. That year, because of Depression-related work shortages, he and many other unfortunates were laid off.

Unemployed, with a growing family to support, Dad had to apply to the city for welfare to assure the family's survival, which was granted. A white resident, viewing this as an affront to his warped sense of fairness, went posthaste to the city fathers and complained bitterly that they were feeding a bunch of Indians. The fathers agreed, and reacted with the proper indignation of bigots. So, in late November of 1935, my parents and their five small children had assistance cut off, were rounded up and deported by the city council from Saint John to Shubenacadie Indian Reserve, Nova Scotia, a place they had never seen before.

Upon their arrival at Shubenacadie Reserve, with little assets other than the clothes on their backs and with cold weather setting in, the Indian Agent gave them a roll of tarpaper and told them to build a tarpaper shack. They did, spending more than two years living in it before moving to the tiny log cabin where I was born.

The reason I mention the circumstance about how I came to be born on Shubenacadie Indian Reserve is to provide an example of the extent of the racism that First Nations Peoples had to contend with at that time. Without any human and civil rights laws to protect us, we were at the mercy of a largely uncaring biased white Anglo society. Therefore, legal redress wasn't available. Factually, the justice system was used by society more to persecute than to dispense justice to us. From birth, as Indians, we were classified as "Wards of the Crown" and, at best, treated as third-class citizens. We had the same legal status in Canada as drunks and insane persons.

Related to the humiliation that my own and other Mi'kmaq families, as well as other minority groups in this country, have suffered because of racial discrimination, I became, with the passage of time, an ardent spokesperson and activist for human rights. I'll use a few more examples to emphasize the extent of the degradation that pushed me to work harder to realize positive change. The following is a short description of how it was growing up as a Registered Indian in those days.

Growing up a Mi'kmaq in Nova Scotia in the 1940s was to know humiliation at almost every turn. This was so because racial discrimination against Registered Indians throughout Canada was overt and widely practiced. Many places were off limits to us because of our race, and there were Canadian laws that segregated us from the general public. Employment was scarce – our people were the last ones hired and the first fired. However, although they were discriminated against when it came to employment opportunities and were forced by circumstances beyond their control to live mostly on meagre welfare handouts, they were labelled by the society that excluded them "lazy Indians."

Racial exclusion was public policy. As "Wards of the Crown," we were not permitted to vote in federal and provincial elections, not permitted in poolrooms, not allowed to have alcoholic beverages internally or externally, and so on. In schools, we were taught that we were from inferior savage cultures and that we had to adopt the "civilized" ways of the white man if we ever wanted to be successful. This is what I was taught at Indian Day School on the Shubenacadie Reserve.

Actually, some of our people did give up their Indian rights in the beliefs that they might be accepted as equals by Canadian society. Instead, they wound up as dirt poor excluded Indians living off reserve – barred by law from living on Indian Reserves. Of course, the idea that we had to give up our culture and adopt one supposedly superior created among First Nations Peoples a massive inferiority complex, and the consequent lack of self-confidence that still hampers their hopes of living in prosperity in Canada today.

The incident that was very instrumental in propelling me to become a determined human rights activist in adulthood happened in the 1940s. For background information, the following is a 1940 food ration memo from the Superintendent of Indian Affairs in Ottawa to Indian Agents, detailing the meagre list of foods available to us.

Scale of Monthly Rations for Indian Relief

No. of Adults	1	2	3	4	5	6
Ration	Lbs.	Lbs.	Lbs.	Lbs.	Lbs.	Lbs.
Flour 2nd grade	24	36	49	61	80	98
Rolled Oats	6	9	12	15	18	18
Baking Powder	1	1¾	1¾	2	2	2
Tea	1	1½	2	2	2	3
Sugar	2	4	5	7	8	10
Lard	3	5	8	10	10	13
Beans	5	5	7	7	8	8

Rice	*2*	*3*	*5*	*5*	*7*	*7*
Cheese	*1*	*1½*	*1½*	*2*	*2*	*3*
Meat or Fish	*$1.00*	*$1.50*	*$1.75*	*$2.00*	*$2.00*	*$2.25*
Salt	*.10 or .15 per month per family*					
Matches	*.10 to .20 per month per family*					

NOTE: Indians under the age of 12 years shall be considered children, and over that age as adults. Issues of rations for each child, of flour, rolled oats, sugar, lard, beans, rice, cheese and meat or fish, shall be one half of the ration for an adult.

Departmental approval must be secured for special rations recommended by the Medical Health Officer in cases of sickness, and milk that may be necessary in the case of infants.

Storekeepers should be warned that if they vary without authority the items contained in this list they are subject to immediate removal from the list of firms authorized to do Government Business. [These rations were purchase orders made out to specific stores whose owners were affiliated with the political party in power.]

Because milk required special approval and resulted in inadequate calcium in our diets when we were young, most children of Registered Indians born up to the early 1950s, including me, have lost their teeth.

Reviewing again the "generosity" that Indian Affairs displayed in its memo to Indian Agents, ordering that subsistence sustenance rations be provided to Registered Indians, rekindles bitter memories in me. I'll describe just one of them.

When I was four or five years old, in 1942 or 1943, Dad had found a job, a twenty-mile or so one-way walk away from home, and would not get paid until the following week. We ran out of food on Friday and had to go without over the weekend. Early Monday morning Mom and I walked the three miles to the Indian Agency where she asked the well-fed agent for a special ration.

Before long the agent had her begging and crying. Then he told her she would have to wait while he thought it over. At about 11:50, ten minutes before his lunchtime, he called us in and gave Mother a two-dollar special order, but not before subjecting her to more humiliating verbal abuse. I remember the event so well for two reasons. First, I was so hungry I could have literally eaten a raw porcupine. Second, it was on that day I made up my mind that when I grew up no one would ever do to me what that bastard had done to my mother – not without a fight. To this day no one ever has.

In the early 1950s, when I was fourteen, halfway through grade eight, without parental permission I took my lack of self-esteem, which had been instilled in me by the education I received in Shubenacadie Indian Day School, to Boston to find work. I was a classic case of the hillbilly going to town. How green I was, and how unprepared for the big city, is exemplified by this incident. When walking down the street for the first few weeks I greeted everyone with a hearty "Good day." The people responded by eyeing me as if I had three heads. I still smile when I think of it.

It was a few years later when I firmly resolved to try to change things for the better for Registered Indians. It happened when I was around nineteen. I was working in a hat factory. Stemming from our chats and my demeanour, it became crystal clear to an African-American woman from Mississippi that I had been conditioned by white society to believe that all Caucasians were better than I was. She called me over one day and gave me a good talking to. These words I'll remember always: "Boy, you're as good as them, and probably better than most of them. Get your head up off the floor and be proud of who you are." No one could have said it better.

I took her advice and began to explore the actual history of the Mi'kmaq and other people of colour residing in Canada and the United States. This was not an easy task because most of the historical information available at that time was written by Caucasians and was very Eurocentric. However, after I had read a lot of it, and between the lines, it soon became clear to me that the history being taught about racially persecuted people in both countries was mostly demonizing lies.

After working in the States for seven years, I came to the conclusion that I would have to improve my education if I wanted to succeed in life. The production line and other factory labour held no further attraction for me.

Thus, at twenty-one, I returned home to Nova Scotia and enrolled in Truro's Success Business College, graduating in 1961 as a bookkeeper. This happened in spite of the Indian Agent telling me, when I applied for education assistance, that "you should do what you're most suited for: get a pick and shovel." Consequently, I've completed many upgrading courses and acquired a grade twelve equivalency certificate. But, mostly, I'm self-taught, and a graduate of the University of Life.

My employment and voluntary experience covers a wide range of activities. My employment includes periods in manufacturing, construction, accounting, and public service. In 1971, I began a fifteen-year stint with the Canadian government's Department of Indian Affairs (as of May 2011, known as the Department of Aboriginal Affairs and Northern Development), holding many positions. During my last five years with the department, I was the Nova Scotia District Superintendent of Lands, Revenues and Trusts. In 1986, at the request of six Band Councils, I left the security of the Federal Public Service and founded for them the Confederacy of Mainland Mi'kmaq. I was the organization's executive director until 1994, when, because of health issues, I decided to try something new.

In my voluntary activities, I served for five years on the Nova Scotia Human Rights Commission. As well, I have been a member of the Nova Scotia Justice System Restructuring Task Force, President of the Micmac Native Friendship Centre, former Chair of the Nova Scotia Department of Education's Mi'kmaq Education Advisory Council, and a board member of the Mi'kmaq Governance Committee.

Today, I occupy myself by writing, lecturing in schools and other public and private entities, run a small advisory business, and write occasional columns for newspapers. A Justice of the Peace for the Province of Nova Scotia and a board member of the Nova Scotia Police Commission, I am also involved in video and radio anti-racism programs, and an avid promoter of human rights and freedoms at every opportunity.

Although not a graduate of a teaching school, I consider myself a teacher. Such was preordained by my experience with racism in my youth. I have, with the passage of time, become more determined to use every educational tool at my disposal to change things for people victimized by intolerance and, where appropriate tools were not available, invent them for the purpose.

I'm a total convert to Michael Levine's philosophy as expressed in his book *Lessons at the Halfway Point: Wisdom for Midlife*: "If you don't personally get to know people from other racial, religious or cultural groups, it's very easy to believe ugly things about them and make them frightening in your mind."

The dream of a decent world for all humanity to live out their lives in peace and prosperity does not have to be a dream. It *is* possible – if we can find the generosity to wisely use the intellect that the Great Spirit gave us to make it a reality.

Sunset Rose Morris

Sunset (Walquasiet) Rose Morris, from Gold River, Nova Scotia, has written three chapbooks for readers of all ages: *Our Storytellers*, *Stick People 1* and *Stick People 2*.

She received her Bachelor of Social Work degree from Dalhousie University and served as the social worker for the Acadia Band reserves. Upon her retirement, she coordinated the mawiomis (gatherings) for fifteen years. Her image was included in Nance Ackerman's recent exhibition, *Wathahine – Photographs of Aboriginal Women*.

Sunset Rose Morris believes we are all healers and she uses her storytelling as building blocks, for they hold many treasures to be absorbed, to be remembered, and to be preserved. Mi'kmaw folks have a long tradition of bringing stories from silent places. She is proud to carry on this tradition. She is also proud to be part of contributing works with other storytellers and poetry writers that can be valued by readers from all nations.

A Woman Am I

Walking in the early morning sun
Positive forces all around me
Leading me to proudly carry on
Hay ya hay ya ho. A woman am I

I am your Mother the earth
I give you food, medicines and more
And now I ask of you, my children
Take away my hurt and my pain
Clean the air we breathe so freely
Clear your spirits and your minds
So the medicines I give you each season
Can be shared with the future generations' children

Did you close your ears to Elders' words?
Did you disobey our Mother Nature's plan?
Fishes die at tidal shores
And the storm's anger purifies
Voluntary outbreaks of flames they strike
The trees bow their heads in mistrust
Unlock my hands – I use them to heal
Untie my hands that I can beat my drum.

Silhouette Lady Blue

There are many countless steps
To where I must go
On daily vision quests
Where amber flowers they grow
Gracefully she reaches high
Dancing delicately so serene
And the eagle. And the eagle screams

Four shining bright walls
I reach out in silent calls
I step forward to Silhouette Lady Blue
There's but one star
And a shadow moon
Silently I reach her space
Slowly she turns
Greets me with a smile
From a crystal mirror I hear her say
My name is Sunset
Roses bloom everywhere
My name is Walquasiet
An eagle feather circles in the air.

My Grandfather

What is your advice to me at this moment, Grandfather?
In my mind's eye, you begin to bring words;
You stand back, you smoke your pipe, you ponder.
The sound of the river flow is waiting in silence with me,
And the fluttering of crows' wings flying above my head.
Then I see my daddy's face on your brown reflection.
In your silent gaze there are many stories.
Created and spared are words to be born, and I listen.
Go to a special place, where there is a cloudy winter day
Where I once stood and resided on a sacred hill.
Many times I conversed with nature, a long time ago.
Pine trees, back and forth they did swing, bowed to me all day
    long.
Whispers I heard, while a pile of wood shavings gathered around
    my aging feet.
Whittling to carve out a wooden maple figure,
A totem face of an elder woman comes into my waiting view.
Carving an eagle feather on her hand, with a few puffs of smoke
    from my pipe I stare and study her.
I then blow some smoke at a bee; it flies away quickly.
I hold the totem in my hands, and give her a name.
I call her Sunset. I pick a flower from a bush nearby.
In my wigwam and beside me is an elderly Mi'kmaq woman and a
    rose.
I say to you, do not put aside or hide your Mi'kmaq beliefs,
For they are not intended to go away ever.
The culture you hold: dream, stay within your heart and your
    mind.
Pass it on, and someday you will paint an image of a totem, give
    it a name and treasure it.
I thank you, Grandfather. Wela'lin.

Silence

What is silence?
Silence does not speak words.
It never leaves your side.
But it is there whenever you need it,
And you ponder: where did it come from?
At my beck and call it will come to me.
Again I ask, where did it come from?
In my own quietness I wait,
What am I waiting for? Silence.
A phantom like invisibility's soul?
Is it related to the wind? No, wind is not silent.
Is it related to the clouds? No, clouds can be seen.
Is it related to time? Ah, now I ask.
And yet I wonder again, and discover at this moment,
Silence is with me surrounding, hovering and awaiting for myself, asking.
Awaiting for a response that I may loudly speak or whisper or ever think about,
And yet, in a crowded area with loud deafening sound surrounding me,
I can be in my own silence where I see or hear no one, but feel my wanting silence.
It surrounds me while my thoughts quickly travel.
I hear no one, I see no one and yet I do not hear or see my silence.
So now, everyone has their own silence.
To me it is a gift, it is medicine, it is a part of me, it never leaves me.

My Island

Surrounded by stones, and flat heavyweight rocks
Where many years past, my island was a bed for a majestic pine tree.
Imagining a wild deer feeding and protecting its young so very new.
On my island, there may be a squawking squirrel catching a sight of me,
As I circle to admire the tiger lilies and roses
That never fail to bloom at many seasons of early springtime.
So very suddenly a piercing thunder startles me,
And a bright flash of lightning rightly follows.
Then you will find me running for shelter from the sudden cool rainfall.
I have but a few years to reach my front door, while a gusty wind blows off my hat.
Another blast of rolling thunder, as I stumble against the door.
By this time I am soaked from the rain; at last the spring shower passes.
Cedar, spruce, fir and maple trees have taken over my small island.
But the flowers grow, showing off their yearly sweet beauties even more.
Storms may come and go, and the winds will forever blow.
Just a tiny piece of ground, surrounded by rocks and stone, is what I call My Island.

Kitpu – The Eagle

There he stands proudly, across the riverbank,
Casting a dark green shadow on the surface of the flowing river.
The trunk of a pine tree, there to hold two large-sized stones
    – Grandfathers.
And it seems as though a nudge would have the riverbank swallow
    the stones.
I leave the riverbank and stagger on rough terrain to reach safer
    ground.
Thirty yards later, I look back and I see the most beautiful eagle
    with her majestic wholeness
Staring at me, adjusting and readjusting her position on the pine
    tree branch.
At a far-off distance to my left, I see a hunter with his gun.
He kneels down on one knee and aims at the eagle, and I scream.
There is a gun blast and I scream, "No!"
Fly away, Kitpu. Another blast, then I hear swish, swish over my
    head.
I look up. Kitpu flies right above me.
Shivers running up my spine, I see the eagle's eye, and her giant
    wings hovering over me.
I imagine the wings are like two black blankets that can easily lift
    me and carry me far, far away.
But not so.
The symbol of the native spirituality – Kitpu – escaped from
    danger.
I witnessed her escape, the beauty and bravery of an eagle I hold
    dear.
There I see Kitpu rising high, screaming at her prey, to be caught
    for a well-deserved meal.
In her orange-coloured beak I see a fish as the morning sun glitters
    on its scales like tiny stars.
Clouded blue sky above and the rocky mountain give me a clearer
    view of Kitpu.

She speeds to her destination for a feast.
I find a shortcut path to my wigwam.
Across the river, the pine tree waves his branches
Holding against his trunk the two large stones I call Grandfathers.
And his shadow on the river doing the same.
I hold my breath and sigh.
For a short moment I wish,
I wish that, like Kitpu, I could fly.
I would fly way back to my ancestors' time,
When each season of living
Spoke to us about how to love ourselves with nature.
Nature is to care, share, provide and inspire.
Similar to Kitpu's never-ending tasks.

The Mountaintop

I am standing atop one of the tallest mountains in the world.
Just me and the mountain's cold, rough winds.
No trees to protect me from harsh, cruel breezes.
No one to talk to but the never-ending wind.
The one form of warmth is my own body heat.
My travel to this nature-made highest monument came from a
 night vision's quest,
In a dream world where impossible things are made possible.
And humans' wishes battle every cause, with efforts from night's
 consciousness.
I have reached that point where I am standing at the mountaintop.
Breathing that's heavy and demanding dries my throat for food and
 water.
I begin to shiver from the mountaintop coldness.
To my left there is an opening amidst the boulder-ice edge.
Enter the cave, I tell myself, in my polar bear lined parka.
Not knowing this was no sweet dream.
But my body heat is one gift that never left me in my dream
 travel.
My thirst is remedied by eating fresh falling snow.
I begin to talk to the ghostly sounding mountain wind.
I ask the wind to bring me food.
The wind says, I cannot bring you food.
I ask the silence to bring me some nourishment.
The silence says, I cannot do that for you.
I ask the cold to bring me bread.
The cold says, I cannot do it ever.
I ask the large icicles, bring me hot tea.
The icicle says, it is impossible for me to grant your request.
Eating snow keeps away the hunger for a while.
Now I ask the lingering fog to bring to me a big red apple.
The lingering fog shakes its head with a gesture of no.
My hungering stomach aches for a hearty and tasty meal.

I fight the cold, but I cannot deal with an empty stomach.
Leaving this ice-cold small cave, I jump to my feet and rush to
    leave.
I stumble over a transparent icicle. Quickly I'm awoken.
And find myself in the real world from whence I came.
Shivering, I go to my kitchen and I eat and eat and I eat again.
If there are human tracks on the mountaintop,
I claim them! They are mine.

Picking Sweet Grass

Way down in the swampy green meadow,
On a hot, muggy midsummer day,
I make my way to the shiny tall grass
That Mother Earth grew for many Mi'kmaq.
This is the place where I pick sweet grass.
I hold my hands above the grassy field.
As I trudge along the soft meadow ground,
I feel the soft swampy black earth under my feet.
Then I offer tobacco in thanksgiving to the Creator.
Crumbled up dry sage leaves, I offer to our Mother the Earth.
With whispered words I say thank you.
Early morning July sun is rising,
And I hear our Mi'kmaq ancestors drumming softly.
I begin to pick one strand at a time.
Humming an ancient Mi'kmaq chant, I break the silence that
    surrounds me.
Picking hundreds of sweet grass strands,
I know the Ancient Ones of our past also picked at this very spot.
To be here on this day I can say that I am following their
    footsteps,
For in my vision I see many Mi'kmaq Elders braiding by the fire to
    pray.
Tiny hummingbirds swarm about, while the eagle squeals way up
    above.
I carry my bundle of swamp-grown sweet grass to my home,
Then I build a fire and braid until the wee hours of the next
    sunrise.

NORTH WINDS AND THE SEA

North winds blow, following the thunder blast.
On my island, by open sea, on a rock, I stand.
Bravely facing the north direction, I sigh.
Displaced by the chilly harsh breeze,
I place one more Indian blanket over myself.
Wild opened sea waves splash against my feet.
Seabirds scream as they fly all around me.
Wind gusts attempt to blow away my blanket hood.
I hear music and whispers in the untamed waves.
Some disturb me, while others haunt me.
Rushing foams twirl and turning waters threaten to hit me with
    ocean cold thrusts.
Another wave sets me off my feet, and
I rush toward the sandy bank, breathless.
I grasp a twig for support, which quickly breaks,
Falling to the ground, I cough and scoff.
For the sea sand weighs heavy on my wet clothes.
A large clamshell appears on my lap,
The seagulls give way to earsplitting cries.
I lift myself quickly off the ground,
And the waves make music and they whisper.
I hear clearly melodies that they bring.
Brushing away a seashell from my soaked lap,
I shiver, but not from the sea-cold.
Saltwater air and winds from the north,
Are met with unsuspecting floating fog.
I now must leave this intriguing seaside
My vehicle is fifty feet from me.
I drive home, wet, cold, and satisfied
After spending time with north winds and the sea.

RESIDENTIAL SCHOOL GONE FOREVER

I am crow clan, I walk away from you.
Black shawl and beaded moccasins,
Take me away, far, far away.
My peaked hat and one crow feather
Lead me to where I must go now.
Over rocks, sand, and green grass I tread
Many crows flying all around me,
And I sit and rest on a fallen spruce tree.
Forever gone, residential schools mistreatments
Disappearing never to return
Then the night falls, the owl bravely stares.
As the night falls, so do the mistreatments.
A new day gives a new birth.
Holding my crow feather I give thanks
Celebrating a birth, I drum and sing with the wind.
Forgiving wholeheartedly was my talk
Upside downs are now rightside ups.
I dance to the beat of my own drum once more,
Crows doing the crow hop delight.
The sharp sound of my handmade whistle
Travels in the green forest far,
And returns to me like a faint shadow
Crows are aplenty, many crows hover wildly.
Residential schools gone forever.
The colourful beads on my moccasins gleam in the sunlight.
As I walk slowly on, my tracks on the ground
Tell many stories that were confined.

A Still Disturbance

You stare at me, and stare I too.
Within ebony – night silent moments.
I come to you for you cannot do the same
On a moment's touch, and step by step with my beaded moccasin feet,
I slowly stride, through white-grey stumps and tall trees
The shawl on my back caught by unseen thorns
Holding me back momentarily.
Snuggled in my long red gown, I feel protected.
Nightingales' melodies travel with me.
I begin to see a silver flash.
The awareness of you, feels the awareness of me.
Brushing away untamed thick branches
We meet once more. A hundredth time
You a bright silver night glow,
You created from a low whispered twilight spray.
Your radiance and charm touch my spirit self
Glittering sparkles of a million tiny stars encountered
I come to see you, as many times before.
But this time are you gone, lost, forever?
No. A low whispered twilight spray reintroduces
And stays with me to unlock my view.
We have moved a giant massive object.
We have moved a mountain.
The heaviness, disappointments and sadness are gone.
Nothing and no one will again blind me.
I see you daily, I see you in my dreams.
Your radiance and your charm
Sparkle and invigorate me.

Lindsay Marshall

Lindsay Marshall is Mi'kmaq and lives on Chapel Island (Potlotek) in the Bras d'Or Lakes (Pitupa'q, which means "flowing into oneness"), where he enjoys spending time on his Tanzer 26 sailboat. Potlotek, a National Historic Site, is known as the Capital of the Mi'kmaq Nation and the home of the Sane' Mawiomi or the Mi'kmaq Grand Council. Lindsay has a son, David Robert Marshall, and two step-daughters. His partner, Mary Louise Bernard, has two daughters, Ashley and Michelle, and one grandchild, Karmalyn Rose.

Lindsay served in the Canadian Armed Forces early in his career and was a deckhand on a supply ship in the Sable Island area. He has also worked as a fire chief and for the water and sewer utility. He began his career in politics in 1988 when he was first elected Band Councillor for Potlotek, serving until 1996. From 1996 until 2002 he was Chief. Lindsay worked for Enterprise Cape Breton for two years and then became Potlotek Chief Executive Officer. In 2006 he became the Associate Dean of the Mi'kmaq College Institute at Cape Breton University. In 2008 he was re-elected as Band Councillor and was subsequently re-elected in 2010 for a further two-year term with the primary portfolio for Education for the community. Presently, he is the principal of Unama'ki

College of Cape Breton University, which was created in July 2010. Lindsay published a collection of poems, *Clay Pots and Bones*, in 1997. In 2010, he had the honour of being commissioned to write a poem, "Kw'aq Pjila'si," for Queen Elizabeth II and to present it to her during her visit to Nova Scotia.

Little Girl Holding a Rose

Little Indian girl holding a rose
looks into the eye of the camera
never questioning the eye
looking back and some say
is stealing her soul.
She holds the namesake of her mom
and her father's mom.
Mother, I know now
what you meant,
I see now what you foretold
and I am saddened
that we ran out of time.
Out of time and out of words
in our awkward past
when we had the chance.
No one jumped to ask;
we just waited for
questions that went unanswered.
Footsteps sink slowly
into soft summer mud
fleeting, not permanent.
Although the clouds
are held at bay,
The wind and rain hover elsewhere.
That is the secret knowledge:
they will come back.
Back to shower us with news
that we may never want to hear.
Unstoppable as the fall of a broken
Branch striking
Mud, raising a puny cloud,
the gentle breeze
carrying it away in protest.

Dust to dust as the white locks
are remembered with pride,
when their colour
matched the bottom
of a pot of tea heated by fire ...

STONES STRIKING FLINT

Seeking game on the Highlands
with our breath frosted
and seeing clouds dance by
as if we were in a place far removed,
above it all.
Crisper and lighter the air swirls
and as the wind pushes us
gently side to side.
How we stood in the Fall's
shadows and waited
as silent as watching a tree grow,
we stood.
We strain for his voice calling us,
great antlers shiny
and the legs standing in water.
We talked with our eyes
and gestured with our faces
but we understood each other's messages.
The light fades and the day's labours
are finished.
Now is the time to rest,
to sit back on a seat
of soft green moss
and a hard upright boulder
caressed by time.
A new day comes
and we are still on the trail,
the signs are fresh
and we picture him standing here
in all of his magnificence
with eyes searching.
Dawn catches him bathing
in the full light of day.

He is closer now
and stands ready.
Slowly he is leaving,
walking toward the distant shore,
and then the light is touching water,
catching each drop,
forming a rainbow.
Little splashes seem
as if they were stones striking flint,
sparking, becoming frequent
till we see signs, fresh,
as if he was still standing here ...

For my brother Kevin Warner

Trapped in Metal Oxide

I hear their voices trapped in metal oxide
former wonder of the universe
back in 1970 something
Oh, the time
when we thought
we would be around
till the ice age came back.
No one is saying that anymore.
No one is saying much anymore
in their now forked tongue.
They claim their status and cheap gas
never knowing why?
Why!
They shout to get in the queue
and when they do they fail to finish.
Failure is an option.
No one thought it would
stay the same;
waiting in a two cyclical schedule
too short for the moon's cycles
but perfect for the government's.
We go back to the metal oxide tape,
our kin predicting the mess
we made.

Freeing Minds

My Elder's voice soothes my troubled soul.
Wise words wash over me,
With gentle movements full of grace
and purpose, he stands.
As sage and sweet grass envelop him
he stands and cleans
our souls and spirits.
Eagle feather in hand,
hair braided with an intricate design.
His weathered hands
fan the flames so they catch
a plume of fire and
sacred smoke slowly takes shape
like a shape-changing
secret entity.
His smudge shell sways
as he begins the process of
prayer and chant,
warming hearts
freeing minds,
voices trailing until silence.

Rain

It washes Mother Earth's cheeks
and washes her tears away, washing away
the pain of the past and present.
The trees stand with their branches
resigned to the weight of the world
for they know the future,
their limbs outstretched.
Wind whispers your name
and passes it on to the
Creator who will hold
you in an infinite loving
embrace.

Gentle Warrior Woman

Sleep, my gentle woman.
Let all know you've won your battles
Using wisdom, spoken words and your gentle soul.
You've moved me, taught me and given me
A love of words.
Step into your birch canoe
And push away from shore.
See the whirls as your paddle moves you
Across land and water.
The sun in its orange and clear sky
Grows larger as you point your kwitn
Towards our Grandfather the sun.
When you reach the farthest shore
Remember us, speak of us
And pray for us
Gentle warrior woman.

I Wrote, Now You Write

Rita Joe

I want to write, but I have to wait
Until my medicine works.
The tremor then stills
The creating has to be freewill, no fear.
I used to be afraid, held back.
Do not step on toes, I was told.
But one must step on toes
If you see something incorrect.

It has been a while since I saw
But the door is still open
This time I'm asking you to help
If you see something that is not right
By all means, point it out
There will always be somebody who cares
Enough to put it right again.

We do not need the humiliation
Like in my time, even as near as in the seventies.
My children knew I was working on culture
So brought what they did not like
Attestment, it would say, rather than the negative.
The only way I knew to fight it
Write the beauty I knew and saw
Even sensed.

It has been done, now you do

LORNE A. JULIEN

The art on the cover of this book is a painting titled *Love Dance* by Mi'kmaq artist Lorne A. Julien. Lorne is from Truro, Nova Scotia, and specializes in original First Nations acrylic paintings. A self-taught artist, he began his craft as a young child. Lorne uses bright colours and believes simplicity is beautiful. His images are of different birds, since they represent freedom in flight. Eagles are his favourite subject material as they are well respected among his people for their ability to fly highest towards the Creator. Receiving an eagle feather is considered an honour for anyone.

Lorne's Mi'kmaq name is Warrior on the Hill, given to him in his youth when he learned about the spiritual ways of his people. He wants to share his artwork, lifting people's spirits, with ideas taken from his visions and dreams. About four years ago he began a Christian journey, wishing to honour Christ in his paintings. Prayers always precede his work. Moreover, Lorne believes he can minister to Native people through his art. As a First Nations person, he feels it is important to tap into traditional Aboriginal skills and life teachings. He also wishes to inspire youth to overcome the restrictions of the past and build on the future, creating healthy communities.

Recently completed work includes *Jesus to the Nations* – an image of an eagle, representing four cultures, and available in limited edition print – and *Relationships*, two eagles above each other, depicting respect for elders and children. Lorne wishes to honour all cultures in his paintings.